VILLAGE JOURNEY

VILLAGE

THE REPORT OF THE ALASKA

BY THOMAS

NEW YORK

A division of

JOURNEY

NATIVE REVIEW COMMISSION

R. BERGER

HILL AND WANG

Farrar, Straus and Giroux

Library of Congress Cataloging-in-Publication Data
Berger, Thomas R.
    Village Journey.
        1. Indians of North America—Alaska—Land tenure.
2. Eskimos—Alaska—Land tenure. 3. Indians of North
America—Alaska—Government relations. 4. Eskimos—
Alaska—Government relations. 5. Indians of North
America—Alaska—Claims. 6. Eskimos—Alaska—Claims.
I. Alaska Native Review Commission. II. Title.
E78.A3B47 1985   979.8′00497   85-17692

For Beverley,

who made the journey with me

PREFACE

In July 1983, the Inuit Circumpolar Conference, an international organization of Eskimos from Alaska, Canada, and Greenland, appointed me to conduct the Alaska Native Review Commission to review the Alaska Native Claims Settlement Act of 1971. The World Council of Indigenous Peoples, an international organization of Native peoples, co-sponsored the commission.

My task took me to Native villages all over Alaska to hear the evidence of Alaska Natives—Eskimos, Indians, and Aleuts. The Native people who gave evidence spoke with great conviction and were concerned that I should understand clearly what they had to say. In this book I have tried to tell their story.

Some persons are skeptical of the Natives' claim to a special attachment to their land. They are worried by the fact that the Native peoples believe in self-determination and a just settlement of their land claims rather than letting themselves be quietly assimilated. At the other extreme, there are persons who romanticize the Natives, trying to discover in them qualities lost by urban residents, and are dismayed when the Natives do not conform to an idealized image.

It has not been easy for the people of village Alaska to be heard. For many years, they have been caught up in the cultural uncertainties of assimilationist policies. Yet I am convinced that in the villages of Alaska I have heard the authentic voice of the Native peoples. I have tried to capture it in this book.

Although I could not hold hearings in every village in Alaska, people from nearby villages came to testify at the hearings in the villages I did get to. The result is that I heard from witnesses from almost every village in Alaska.

Throughout *Village Journey* I refer to the Eskimo, Indian, and Aleut peoples collectively as Natives, though each of them is a distinct people that includes many subgroups. Among the Eskimos of Alaska, two main languages, Inupiat and Yup'ik, are both widely spoken. In many Indian villages, the Native tongue is still in use. Some Athabascan Indians of interior Alaska speak their languages, and some Indians in southeast Alaska speak Tlingit, Haida, and Tsimshian. Some people of the Aleutian Islands speak Aleut. All testimony given in the Native languages was translated for me. I have tried to follow Native peoples' preferences for spelling, but, to avoid confusion, I have used the same word to designate both culture and language (e.g., Athabascan, Inupiat, Yup'ik). In the spelling of names like Athabascan, or umiat, I have adopted the usages of Native people in Alaska. So also in the usages regarding a person's names; e.g., George Jim, Sr. I have also followed the custom in Alaska by using "Alaska" as an adjective; e.g., "Alaska Natives."

Where I mention witnesses who hold office of any kind, I refer to the office held when that person testified. Only a few acronymns appear: ANCSA (Alaska Native Claims Settlement Act, 1971), ANILCA (Alaska National Interest Lands Conservation Act, 1980), AFN (Alaska Federation of Natives, Inc., a statewide organization of the Native regional corporations), UTA (United Tribes of Alaska, a statewide organization of tribal governments), and IRA (the Indian Reorganization Act).

I use the terms "Whites" and "White people" to mean Western man and the representatives of industrialized society generally, a context in which "White" may include persons of other colors. I have chosen this expression because, throughout the hearings, Alaska Natives referred to "the White man" and "White people." They knew whom they meant, and so do we. Occasionally, I use the word "we" to mean the White population of North America and to remind readers that I share the culture, perceptions, and experience of the White majority.

No one, in a single book—or in a single lifetime—could hope to unravel the complexities of issues that have beset White-Native relations ever since Columbus made his landfall in the West Indies in 1492. We know, however, that these issues are still with us and that we—and the Native people—must come to grips with them.

My journey to the villages of Alaska was an inner journey as well. Any inquiry into the condition of the Native peoples, any discussion of their goals and aspirations, must also entail a consideration of our own values. What we learn in this process about Native society should teach us much about our own society.

No enterprise that requires travel and the hearing of testimony all over Alaska could be undertaken without the help and dedication of many persons. David S. Case served as commission counsel, Rosita Worl as special consultant, Mary Kancewick as special counsel, Eileen Panigeo MacLean as village liaison, Jim Sykes as documentary sound engineer, Don Gamble first and Dorik Mechau later as coordinator, Joyce Johnson as office manager, Wanda Keller as office secretary in Anchorage, Val Chapman as office secretary in Vancouver, Thelma Ingrim as accountant, Alan Cooke as copy editor, and Judith Brogan as managing editor. Dawn Scott handled the word processing. I should also acknowledge the advice and assistance of Professors Thomas Lonner and Steve Langdon of the University of Alaska, Anchorage; Professor Bart Garber of the University of Alaska, Fairbanks; Professor Ralph Johnson of the University of Washington; Professor Charles Wilkinson of the University of Oregon; David Getches, Executive Director of the Colorado Department of Natural Resources; Robert T. Coulter of the Indian Law Resource Center, Washington, D.C.; Reid Chambers of Washington, D.C.; Professor Douglas Sanders of the University of British Columbia; Professor Ted Chamberlin of the University of Toronto; Vernita Zilys of Rural Alaska Community Action Program; and Charles Smythe of Chilkat Institute. I thank them all.

Dalee Sambo, special assistant to the president of the Inuit Circumpolar Conference, was responsible for raising funds to enable the commission to complete its work. The Alaska Humanities Forum was a steadfast supporter of the commission, and its executive director Gary Holthaus was especially helpful.

Arthur Wang of Hill and Wang, publishers, offered encouragement and advice throughout and I am grateful to him.

Many organizations provided financial support to the commission. The North Slope Borough, under both Mayor Eugene Brower and his successor, George Ahmaogak, made the largest contribution. In addition, the Alaska Humanities Forum, The National Endowment for the Humanities, The Ford Foundation,

Northshore Unitarian Universalist Veatch Program, Rockefeller Brothers Fund, The Rockefeller Foundation, and the Rural Alaska Community Action Program were very generous. Additional contributors include the United Methodist Church, National Program Division; World Council of Churches Program to Combat Racism; Ann Roberts Fund; Rockefeller Family Fund; Kawerak, Inc.; The Prospect Hill Foundation; J. Roderick MacArthur Foundation; Chugach Alaska Corporation; Klukwan, Inc.; Ukpeagvik Inupiat Corporation; Sealaska Corporation; The Wilderness Society; Sunflower Foundation; NANA Regional Corporation; Community Enterprise Development Corporation; Nu Lambda Trust and IBM's Anchorage office; and Mrs. Henry S. Forbes. A multitude of individuals and organizations, too numerous to list here, provided services in kind. I thank them all.

T.R.B.

Anchorage
July 1985

CONTENTS

ILLUSTRATIONS

VILLAGE JOURNEY

Map prepared by Arctic Environmental Information and Data Center, University of Alaska—
Fairbanks

INTRODUCTION

Tununak: a Yup'ik Eskimo village of about two hundred residents on Nelson Island in southwest Alaska. Here, in February 1984, the sun glints low for seven or eight hours each day, then the long night falls again. It is forty degrees below zero, and a bitter wind is blowing off the Bering Sea when we arrive by Twin Otter. In summer, Tununak is a fishing village but now, deep in winter, the people hunt caribou and occasionally they take a musk-ox. A walk across the village against a high wind is an adventure. Bundled in a parka and scarves, it is like wading through surf. During the mid-1970s, I spent three years traveling throughout the Canadian Arctic, but I don't think I've ever been this cold before. The people of both countries are related—Eskimos, whose ancestors fanned out over the circumpolar region from the Bering Sea to Greenland, and Indians, whose ancestors spread out over North and South America. They are distinct races, but both are aboriginal peoples.

I am holding a public hearing in the school gym, and we have a full house. The villagers are sitting on mats and parkas on the gym floor. Some of the older faces, and a few of the younger ones, are scarred by frostbite. Two students from this modern school hold cameras to record our proceedings on videotape. The first language of every child in this village is Yup'ik. The testimony, in both English and Yup'ik, is about land claims, Native corporations, tribal government, and subsistence.

> Our subsistence way of life is especially important to us. Among other needs it is our greatest. We are desperate to keep it. *(Paul John, Tununak)*

The word "subsistence" reminds most Americans of dirt-poor farmers, scratching a hard living from marginal land. In Alaska, however, subsistence means hunting, fishing, and gathering. More than that, it means a way of life that—far from being marginal—fulfills spiritual as well as economic needs.

My job here is to review with the people what the Alaska

Native Claims Settlement Act means to them, what the act (which everyone in Alaska calls ANCSA) has meant to the villagers themselves. Under ANCSA, which the U.S. Congress passed in 1971, an act widely acclaimed as the most generous settlement of aboriginal claims ever made, Alaska Natives would receive $962.5 million and, still more important to them, title to forty-four million acres of land. To the people of Tununak, land is the key to the settlement. To them, the land is their life. Far from securing their land, ANCSA has placed their land at risk.

> We Yup'iks do not wish to lose the land. We would like to use the land as our ancestors did. We would like to use it without any problems. *(Mike Angaiak, Tununak)*

Native people here are proud of their tribal heritage, but Congress did not convey the land to tribal entities. When Congress enacted ANCSA, it considered tribal governments to be an impediment to assimilation. Instead, the law required the Natives to set up village and regional corporations to obtain title to the land. The land that ANCSA conveyed does not belong to Alaska Natives, it belongs to these corporations. Hence, the Native corporations are the most visible structures established under this legislation. But these corporate structures put the land at risk. For Native land is now a corporate asset. Alaska Natives fear that, through corporate failure, corporate takeovers, and taxation, they could lose their land.

At Tununak, I find anger and disbelief. In fact, as I later learned, discontent with ANCSA simmers everywhere in the state. Alaska Natives believe they have been cheated.

> This act was done for our future benefit, but it has hurt us, our children and grandchildren, and those that are yet to be born. If we do not do anything about this, that is exactly our future. *(Mike Albert, Tununak)*

Fort Yukon: an Athabascan village of seven hundred on the Arctic Circle. The Hudson's Bay Company established a trading post here in 1842, when the territory was still part of Russian

America. In the log building used as a museum, the people gather for the hearing among displays of ancient quillwork and modern beadwork. At every village I visit—and, during two years, I visit sixty villages and I hear more than 1,450 witnesses —I reiterate that I do not represent the United States government. I have no mandate from the federal government nor from the State of Alaska to review ANCSA. I am a Canadian, not an American. The Inuit Circumpolar Conference, an international organization of Eskimos from Alaska, Canada, and Greenland, has appointed me to do this work, which the World Council of Indigenous Peoples, an international organization of Native peoples, is co-sponsoring. My working group is called the Alaska Native Review Commission (ANRC). Both of my sponsors are affiliated with the United Nations. Both of them represent indigenous peoples at meetings of international bodies. They have one other thing in common: they are always on the verge of insolvency. So is my commission, yet we are accomplishing our work. Money is coming in from many sources: from churches and foundations, from Native organizations and the Native people. Eskimos at Nome are sending to the commission the proceeds of their weekly bingo games. At every village we visit, the local people arrange a place for us to stretch out our sleeping bags—sometimes there is even a bed. At Fort Yukon, they provided us with a potluck supper and entertained us. We listened to Athabascan fiddlers play far into the night.

Gambell: an Eskimo village on St. Lawrence Island. Here we are closer to Siberia than we are to the Alaska mainland. The people of Gambell are Yup'ik, Siberian Yup'ik, with closer ties to their relatives in Siberia than to the Yup'ik on mainland Alaska. The elders, to whom great deference is shown, speak first; some of them were born in Siberia. Some elderly women have traditional facial tattoos, lines that run from the lower lip to beneath the chin.

Congress wanted Alaska Natives to become shareholders and businessmen, to become part of the commercial and corporate mainstream of America. There are few business opportunities on this windswept island. The people of Gambell are subsistence hunters and fishermen. In spring they hunt bowhead whales, in winter they hunt walrus. It is the land, the island itself and the waters around it, that is their principal concern. If the village corporation fails, for whatever reason, creditors could attach the ancestral land of these villagers. After 1991, shares in the corporation can be sold; after this date, outsiders could take over the village corporation and its assets, including the land. After 1991, the state may tax the land, even though it generates no revenue.

Alaska Natives thought that ANCSA would protect their lands so they could pass them on to future generations. They believed that this "settlement" was precisely that: by ANCSA, Congress had extinguished aboriginal title throughout the state, but it had conceded the Native peoples' right to keep forty-four million acres of ancestral land. Today they find that ANCSA is the very instrument whereby they could lose their land. Nothing, in fact, has been settled.

At Gambell, Paul Apangalook, a man in his early thirties, says:

> I've always believed this island was ours. All that [ANCSA did] was to recognize our ownership. But [three] other things were done: first, the stocks were wedged between the land and its people; second, a profit structure was imposed; third, all of what we gained under the act was under a timetable.

You could travel far, as I have, and you could listen to many lawyers and consultants, as I have, but you will not find a clearer explanation of what ANCSA means. Native understanding of some of its details may often be imperfect, but the people's appreciation of its consequences is sound.

New Stuyahok: a Yup'ik Eskimo fishing village on Nushagak River, near Bristol Bay. The people here depend on the world's largest runs of red salmon. When I was there, during the winter, some of the men were out sealing. It was cold, and children were skating in the icy streets. At the hearing that night, Wally Gust asks:

> Who has ANCSA benefited? You, the Natives? No. It seems to me it benefited non-Natives. We got land, money. Where has it gone? Mostly to well-educated non-Natives, lawyers.

His is a common complaint, and there is much truth in it. One of ANCSA's clauses, which requires division of subsurface revenues among Native corporations throughout the state, has drained an estimated $35 million in legal fees. In at least one region, Kodiak, lawsuits have bled the Native corporations dry.

For most village corporations, the story is a sad one. Undercapitalized, without corporate experience, with virtually no business prospects, the corporations were at the mercy of the lawyers, advisers, and consultants who flocked to the villages like scavengers. Now the money is largely gone, and the land itself is at risk.

The village corporations are legally constituted to make profits, to pursue economic purposes. Yet the villagers themselves are chiefly concerned with subsistence activities. This can place the corporations at cross purposes with their village shareholders. At New Stuyahok, Natalie Susuk offered a view that many witnesses repeated:

> As we all know, these [corporate] officers-representatives were originally chosen for the fact that they would attend to business matters relating to a profit corporation. These representatives may or may not have as much conviction as others on the issues of subsistence living and land retention, which seems to be the main concern of most Natives I know. We shouldn't expect corporation officers to represent our interests.

Fairbanks: Alaska's second-largest city is the headquarters of Doyon, Ltd., the regional corporation of most of the Athabascan Indians living in villages in the interior of the state. Doyon has incurred enormous losses. Every village in the region has expressed intense dissatisfaction with Doyon. It has paid high salaries to its executives (many of whom are non-Natives), but dividends have been minuscule. Once Doyon's prospects seemed bright. I remember visiting the boardroom of Doyon's offices in Fairbanks in 1975, during the early days of ANCSA. It was a showpiece and symbol of the new wealth transferred to Alaska Natives. Doyon, which had received twelve million acres under ANCSA, is the largest private landowner in Alaska.

Doyon may be the state's largest private landowner, but its very size has made it vulnerable. Financial losses have put the title to its vast landholdings at risk. Moreover, because ANCSA gave the subsurface title of village lands to the regional corporations, Doyon's bankruptcy would have grave consequences for every Athabascan village in the region. Doyon's creditors could end up owning the subsurface rights beneath the villages.

For Alaska Natives, ANCSA has been the means of selecting land to be held by the Native corporations and the means by which these corporations have acquired economic power and political influence. This influence is exercised primarily by the regional corporations. For more than a decade now, ANCSA has been celebrated. That celebration has now ended. Although journalists still write in wonderment about Native executives in three-piece suits and about gleaming corporate offices, this evidence is misleading. Behind the façade lies the reality of village Alaska. Sam Demientieff, the new chairman of Doyon, said in his testimony at Fairbanks,

> If you deal with all the problems and if you get to the point where a corporation is successful, making money, there's a lot of things that the corporation can do, and it's a tool that can be used if it is successful . . . [but] the corporation's not, it's not the right answer . . . we have to have something that reflects membership as the Native people go through generations, that they still are members of their tribe or the group that they belong to, the village.

Angoon: a Tlingit Indian village on Admiralty Island in southeast Alaska. It is May, and the villagers are mending their nets. A clutter of homes is scattered along the shoreline. Clan crests, raven, eagle, whale, wolf, are painted on some of the houses. Gabriel George says that "Angoon's well known as the stronghold of Tlingit culture."

We are far away from the Eskimo villages on the Bering Sea and the Arctic coast. Admiralty Island is heavily timbered. Along the shore, two ravens are teasing an eagle. In the woods, you can hear a multitude of bird calls, a squawk from the brush, a long, low twitter far off among the trees.

Alaska is vast, and the Tlingit are quite different from the Yup'ik and the Athabascan. Although they share certain cultural attributes, they are, in fact, several quite different peoples:

Inupiat, Yup'ik, Aleut, Athabascan, Tlingit, Haida, and Tsimshian.

The ancestors of the Inupiat crossed Bering Strait from Asia
thousands of years ago and settled the Arctic coasts from the
Chukchi Sea as far east as Greenland. The Greenlandic Eskimos
speak the same language as the Inupiat of Alaska. In interior
Alaska, along the Yukon and Tanana rivers, live Athabascan
Indians, whose ancestors also came from Asia; the Navajos and
Apaches of Arizona and New Mexico speak a similar tongue. In
southeast Alaska, Tlingit, Haida, and Tsimshian Indians live
from the sea. Their art, adornment, and customs have excited
the admiration of scholars and collectors throughout the world
ever since Whites first visited them more than two hundred
years ago. The coast of southwest Alaska and the deltas of the
Yukon and Kuskokwim rivers are home to some twenty thousand Yup'ik Eskimos, the greatest concentration of Eskimos in
the world. They still depend on hunting, fishing, and gathering.
On the Pribilof Islands and the Aleutian chain, the Aleuts, kin
to the Yup'ik, were decimated by a century and a half of Russian
occupation; they now number no more than a few thousand.
They, too, maintain their own cultural identity.

All of these people in rural Alaska still live mainly from the
land, they are still connected with their ancient values. In the
sixty villages that I visited, I could see that Native values have
been battered, but they are not destroyed. In some villages they
are still powerful and pervasive; in others, they are clearly
diminished. Nevertheless, respect for the wisdom of elders, a
special relationship with the land, an ethic of sharing, the concept of the extended family, and other traditional values persist
in one form or another throughout village Alaska. Ivan Gambell,
president of the Angoon village corporation, testified:

> We had to decide between employment or preserving the area for
> subsistence. . . our board of directors voted to protect the Angoon
> area . . . we hoped the weight of what subsistence provided for us
> would outweigh the need for jobs.

Walter Soboleff, a Tlingit elder and scholar, testified at Angoon: "I'm saying that the basic traditions of our people stand

as living monuments. Around these things, the people endeavored to live with justice, a sense of pride, a sense of dignity, a sense of honor."

Huslia: an Athabascan village of about two hundred residents on Koyukuk River. The village consists of comfortable log houses scattered among the birch and spruce. These homes are heated by wood stoves, not oil furnaces such as you hear thundering in the corner of government-issue prefabs in villages on the tundra. At the hearing, villagers spoke eagerly of their way of life, their dependence on the land. When the hearing was over and after a prayer, we tucked away a potluck meal of moose, beaver, duck, and Indian ice cream (a mixture of berries and fat). The entire village attended. It strikes me once again that the attempt to reproduce corporate America in these small villages is a strange idea.

People bring their children, even their babies, to the hearings. Sometimes a child of three or four will accompany a parent who is testifying to the microphone. Under ANCSA, that child is excluded from the settlement. The parent is a shareholder, but every Native child born since December 18, 1971, the date of ANCSA's passage, is excluded. Natives born since that date have no legal interest in the Native corporations or the Native lands the corporations hold. ANCSA strikes at the heart of the kinship ties that bind together village life in Alaska. Everywhere I went, the people demanded to know why children were excluded from the settlement. This question goes at once to the essence of ANCSA. Children had to be excluded from a profit-making corporate structure.

> The way I see things now . . . [I have] concern about the kids that was born after '71, 1971. I could see now that, if we don't do anything or try to help them, they'll be the people that will be cut off from their land . . . a thing that we cannot live without. And seems like the way things . . . is going . . . it will get to the end where we are not on our own, on our own land, because of too many different urban people's law, which we have not brought up with, which we have not lived with. . . . Our own belief about our land is as strong as urban people's law, but it's not recognized. . . . We have a lot of beliefs. If we have to write or record our beliefs in

Indian way, the way our people lived for hundreds of years, thousands of years, I think it will be as big as a Bible . . . there's times that I begin to think about what it's going to be. It's not for myself but more for my young people, my grandchildrens. *(Katherine Attla, Huslia)*

Unalakleet: an Inupiat Eskimo village on Norton Sound. The people here fish and they hunt walrus and seals. Like most villages in Alaska, Unalakleet is not a place where many Americans would find it easy to live. Although many Alaska Natives have migrated to urban centers, most village populations have increased since the 1960s.

Congress has tried to transform these people by legislation, but it could not transform geography. In only a few cases has ANCSA enlarged opportunities for the villagers. Federal and state funding, not the $962.5 million disbursed by ANCSA, has improved village and household amenities, but at a cost of which everyone is well aware—dependence.

All the things that the White man has brought—language, religion, medicine, schools, welfare—when laid side by side constitute a barrier, walling Native people off from their own past and at the same time from future possibilities. As individuals, some can overcome these barriers, but as a society they cannot. Barriers are continually closing in on them, barriers that seem cunningly devised to limit their range of possibilities. At the hearing in the Unalakleet school gym, Polly Koutchak, a young woman, expresses the frustration felt by many.

I always feel deep within myself the urge to live a traditional way of life—the way of my ancestors. I feel I could speak my Native tongue, but I was raised speaking the adopted tongue of my people, English. I feel I could dance to the songs of my people, but they were abolished when the White man came to our land. I feel I could heal a sick one the way it was done by my ancestors, but the White man not only came with their medicine—they came with diseases. What I'm trying to say and emphasize is I am one in modern day attempting to live a double life—and, from that, my life is filled with confusion. I have a wanting deep within myself to live the life of my ancestors, but the modernized world I was raised in is restricting me from doing so. First, the White man came and abolished our song and dance, then they took control over our land and its resources, and then they shoved us into a life totally unknown to us, expecting us to conform to it irregardless of our knowledge. Although I feel bitterness and animosity, I would like to attempt to bring back what was taken from us as a people.

Tanana: in July, I travel in a small, flat-bottomed river boat along the Yukon River to hold hearings at Indian villages, stopping at fish camps along the way. This is Athabascan country, and everyone seems pleased to see us. At one camp, we sit on logs on the beach and talk about the land claims settlement. ANCSA has not only extinguished aboriginal title to the land, it has also extinguished aboriginal rights of hunting and fishing. State and federal laws now conflict with traditional ways that had the force of law among the Native people. State fish and game regulations are steadily encroaching on Native use of the land and waters. They told me that White fishermen have taken over many of the good fishing places on which the Natives have always depended. All along the Yukon I hear the same complaints, often expressed with deep resentment. Anger is contained—but not always—only by immense restraint. At Lester Erhart's camp, Bobby Kokrine testified:

> Say [a white man] bought a license [limited-entry permit] in Anchorage on this river, they figure they have a right to move into any spot in the country. And I've seen it, Lester's seen it and everybody's seen it just time and time again.

After a week on the river, we reach Tanana, a community of about five hundred, only half of whom are Native. The White population is fully employed. There are few jobs for the Natives, few opportunities for wage employment. Subsistence is vital for the Natives here; subsistence activities are their employment. In village Alaska, the people depend on fish and wildlife: northern agriculture can never replace the harvests from hunting and fishing. Legal regimes now threaten Native access to these fish and wildlife resources.

Akiachak: a village that has been at the center of the Yup'ik Eskimos' movement for self-government. At the hearing, high school students watch while the elders speak about the past and their future. Peter Waska, an older man from nearby Tuluksak, spoke first in English, haltingly, without fluency; then he said, "I speak my tongue." Switching to Yup'ik, he spoke with ease and confidence, he captured his listeners, drawing them into his confidence. Like many others, he spoke of the history of Alaska. Charlie Kairiuak translated:

> He said . . . he's here to talk about ANCSA. . . . They might not like what he has to say but what he says comes from the heart. . . . He said that the Russians did not live here . . . because the Russians were not born here, and they did not own this land, that it was illegal for them to sell it. . . . The Russians sold it like [they] owned it and ignored the real owners . . . the ancestors who originally owned it, way before recorded time . . . [and they] have passed this ownership to the people here. . . . And he said that he does not like outside people doing anything to the state because he feels that they . . . [do] not have the authority to . . . do the things that they do. . . . And that even though he is shy, he is testifying so that what he says can be recorded here, and also elsewhere.

Congress intended ANCSA to integrate the Natives of Alaska into the institutions of Alaska. Under ANCSA, the land in the village itself and immediately around it has to be reconveyed from the village corporations to state-chartered local governments. The people of Akiachak believe that tribal government must be restored. In 1983, they voted to dissolve the state-chartered local government and to transfer its assets to their tribal government. I have observed that the movement for tribal government is gathering strength at the village level throughout the state. Here in Akiachak this movement is furthest advanced.

> We want to have a government-to-government relationship with the state and the federal government . . . we are sovereign people. And we're going to be sovereign as long as we live. And we're going to be working together as one mind to form a Yup'ik nation. *(Jackson Lomack, Akiachak)*

One of the things that keep coming out is that our government has existed since time immemorial. So the government we have, the tribal government, has existed and was a legal government when Columbus supposedly discovered America back in 1492. . . . There has been a crying need to re-establish the tribal government. The government that now exists, specifically the federal government and the state government, is not our way of government, our Yup'ik way of government. The elders are saying, reestablish your tribal governments. Make your own laws, practice your self-determination as your ancestors have practiced it. *(Willie Kasayulie, Akiachak)*

Barrow: the largest Inupiat village in Alaska. Near the tip of Point Barrow, on the Arctic Ocean, with a population of about 2,500, it is the northernmost community in the United States. When I arrived here in August, there was still sea ice floating offshore.

Here on the North Slope is the great oil field at Prudhoe Bay. The effects of oil exploration and development have been more pronounced here than anywhere else in the state. The people in the villages of the North Slope are worried about damage to the habitats of their fish and wildlife resources.

We are . . . dealing with the strong lies of the oil companies in Nuiqsut. They are destructing the hunting grounds within Nuiqsut, in the east side and the west side. Because of the oil companies, there is scarcity of fish and other game animals. There used to be plenty of fish before the oil companies. We grew up in that land before 1920 and we lived there until 1950, and we have returned to that land. There used to be all types of animals, such as caribou, fish, and other game. But they have decreased because of the oil activities! *(Bessie Ericklook, Nuiqsut)*

The new wealth is unwinding the social fabric of the region. Ronald Brower, vice-president of the village corporation, speaks of the pain his people feel:

Oil development is a problem, our people are finding out. . . . We can anticipate that in a few years, maybe twenty or thirty years, the

Arctic Slope . . . will have as many fields developed to the enormity of Prudhoe Bay. They're starting up now in small areas, but cumulatively the total will have devastating impact on our culture, because we are a hunting culture. And that frame of mind has not left our people, even though we have been immersed into a cash economy.

But, when you look at the total package, money has spoken over above all of those, and that money is being used against them. You see, the oil-lease sales taking place in areas where our people have deep, sacred ancestral feelings. Well, oil development in the Arctic is destroying those feelings quite rapidly. You can see it in the loss of language that our younger generations are now experiencing. It's visible in the way our school children living today have an "I-don't-care" attitude. Why should we learn? What's the future of learning? You see generation gaps developing where there never used to be any, and language barriers developing between grandparents, parents, and grandchildren. That is quite evident, all you have to do is approach one of our families. You'll find the eldest, who may speak only Inupiat and, on the other hand, their grandchildren speaking only English. So, we are presently in the Arctic Slope experiencing a very different form of a degeneration of our society, both physically, mentally, economically, spiritually, and culturally. The damage is evident, you just have to look at it.

Port Graham: a village on the tip of the Kenai Peninsula, it is isolated by mountains and by Cook Inlet. Here the Yup'ik and Aleut cultures mix. Wildlife resources are under increasing pressure from the burgeoning urban populations of the Kenai Peninsula and from nearby Anchorage. Natives are being pushed out of the subsistence salmon fishery. The loss of these resources is keenly felt here because of the sale by Natives of limited-entry commercial fishing permits to non-Natives.

To dismiss the sale of these permits and the sale of shares in the Native corporations as a matter of personal choice will not do. Permits and shares alike represent the division of what the Native peoples have always regarded as a common resource into distinct units of individual wealth; these units are passing from Natives to non-Natives. The experience with limited-entry permits suggests that shares in the village and regional corporations will be sold when it becomes possible to alienate stock freely at the end of 1991. As with limited-entry commercial fishing permits, shareholders who sell their stock after 1991 will be making a choice that must affect all of their descendants.

> I worry of somebody's going to be sold. When they are sold out, you sold out your hundred shares, your land, and you can't pass it on to your children. Your children are not going to inherit it. That's the tainted part of the stock—unrestricted—because, for instance, a lot of limited entries being sold all over the state of Alaska, not only on Port Graham, in other villages. It's going to happen, same thing. *(Walter Meganck, Port Graham)*

St. Paul: a cliff-bound island in the Bering Sea with a population of less than five hundred, it is the largest Aleut community in the world. The Russians brought the Aleuts here from the Aleutians in the late eighteenth century to harvest fur seals. They have depended on this harvest ever since, but now they are threatened by the activities of some conservation groups that are trying to stop the harvest of fur seals. It is the only important economic activity in the region; losing the fur-seal harvest may be equated with losing the island.

> We are not begging. We're asking for respect for our land, for our people. We were brought to this island many years ago. Please don't take it from us. *(Olga Merculieff, St. Paul)*

After visiting sixty villages, I know the depth of feeling about the land that exists among the Native peoples of rural Alaska. Throughout the state, they know that under ANCSA their aboriginal rights were extinguished and that many uncontrolled and perhaps uncontrollable forces now threaten their way of life. Their control of their lands is not secure. Alaska Natives wish to choose a form of landholding that reflects their own cultural imperatives and ensures that their ancestral lands will remain in their possession and under their governance. They reject assimilation, and they are determined to fashion a future of their own.

At every hearing, witnesses talk of the corporations, shares, profits, sometimes even of proxies, but then, emerging from this thicket of corporate vocabulary, they will talk of what they consider of most importance to them—land, subsistence, the future of the villages. In this book I must therefore do the same. An analysis of ANCSA will not be sufficient. If I am to do justice to all that I have heard, it will be necessary to address all of these questions.

Alaska Natives now realize that ANCSA has failed them and that its goals are at cross purposes with their own. Today they are trying to strengthen their subsistence economy and to restore their tribal governments. We must understand the historical legitimacy and the present value of these goals. These aspirations are not anachronistic, they are not absurd, they are not an impediment to progress. They are, quite simply, the only means whereby the future well-being of village Alaska can be protected.

I know that many persons deplore the failure of Alaska Natives to embrace the customs, institutions, and world view of their White fellow citizens. In rejecting them, Alaska Natives are not clinging blindly to the past, nor are they stubbornly unwilling to live up to the expectations of Congress. It is their profound desire to be themselves, to be true to their own values, that has led to the present confrontation. Far from deploring their failure to become what strangers wish them to be, we should regard their determination to be themselves as a triumph of the human spirit.

One /

THE PROMISE

OF THE CLAIMS ACT

Congress finds and declares that (a) there is an immediate need for a fair and just settlement of all claims by Natives and Native groups of Alaska, based on aboriginal land claims; (b) the settlement should be accomplished rapidly, with certainty, in conformity with the real economic and social needs of Natives, without litigation, with maximum participation by Natives in decisions affecting their rights and property. *(ANCSA, Section 2(b))*

We had some great hopes in that we would be living a better life as a result of ANCSA and that we would be reaping some of the benefits. That has not been the case. . . . The intentions are good, but it's just not working the way it was intended. *(Ronald Brower, Barrow)*

The Promise

ANCSA was hailed as a new departure for the resolution of aboriginal claims. By its terms, Alaska Natives would have land, capital, corporations, and opportunities to enter the business world. By its terms, Alaska Natives would receive title to forty-four million acres of land and $962.5 million in compensation. By its terms, Alaska Natives were obliged to set up corporations to serve as the vehicles for the ownership and management of this land and the money, which became corporate assets. For twenty years, Alaska Natives would be the only voting share-holders in these corporations.

Congress wanted to bring the Alaska Natives into the mainstream of American life. Senator Henry Jackson, the principal architect of ANCSA, and, indeed, all of the other key figures in Congress, opposed the extension of the Indian reservation system to Alaska. There was opposition, too, among Alaska Natives to the idea of reservations. Congress also rejected the possibility that tribal governments might be used to implement the settlement. Douglas Jones, assistant to Senator Mike Gravel of Alaska when ANCSA was passed, now a professor at Ohio State University, testified that ANCSA was a form of "social engineering." William Van Ness, staff assistant to Senator Jackson at this period, also asserted that "The act was . . . a very radical effort at social engineering and it was done on a very, very calculated basis."

Although Congress recognized the necessity of a land base for the Native subsistence economy, it nevertheless insisted that economic development of the land must become the principal means of improving social and economic conditions in village Alaska. By this means, Congress intended Native people to go into business and to participate actively in the economic development of Alaska. The report that accompanied the final House bill explained that:

> In determining the amount of land to be granted to the Natives, the Committee took into consideration the land needed for ordinary village sites and village expansion, the land needed for a subsistence hunting and fishing economy by many of the Natives, and the land needed by the Natives as a form of capital for economic development.

Congress regarded this last use of the land as paramount.

> The acreage occupied by villages and needed for normal village expansion is less than 1,000,000 acres. While some of the remaining 39,000,000 acres may be selected by the Natives because of its subsistence use, most of it will be selected for its economic potential.

It may seem that forty-four million acres is a great deal of land, and indeed it is. But it should be kept in mind that in 1971 Alaska Natives held aboriginal title to virtually all of Alaska, a title based on Native use and occupation of the land since time immemorial. As George Jim, Sr., said at Angoon, "Who's been here before us? There's nobody but us, our people." During the eighteenth century, Russian fur traders found their way to Alaska. Russian occupation was scattered along the Aleutian Islands, around the Gulf of Alaska, and in southeast Alaska. In

1867, by the Treaty of Cession, Russia sold its interests in Alaska to the United States for $7.2 million.

The discovery of gold in Alaska in 1898, the development of a commercial salmon fishery along the coast between Ketchikan and Bristol Bay, and logging activities in southeast Alaska brought many White settlers into the territory. When the United States declared war on Japan in 1941, the nation was made suddenly aware of Alaska's strategic position. In 1943, Japan invaded the Aleutian Islands, and more than 140,000 American military personnel were sent to Alaska. To serve as a supply route to Alaska, the military built a 1,523-mile gravel highway through Canada to Fairbanks.

Native land claims date back to 1867. Immediately after the sale of Alaska to the United States, the Tlingit Indians of southeast Alaska protested the sale, arguing that they were the owners of the land they occupied. In 1912, the Tanana chiefs asserted their aboriginal title to lands in interior Alaska because of the impingement of White settlers on traditional hunting and fishing activities in the region. In 1935, the Tlingit and Haida sued to establish their aboriginal claim to lands taken from them for Tongass National Forest. In 1959, the Tlingit and Haida secured a judgment in the action they had brought in 1935: they were entitled to compensation for the land taken from them. The U.S. Court of Claims explicitly declared that the Treaty of Cession, 1867, did not extinguish aboriginal title. Finally, in 1968, they were awarded $7.5 million.

When, in 1958, Alaska became a state, the settlement of Native land claims acquired a new urgency. Although the Statehood Act disclaimed any right to land and property held by Alaska Natives or held in trust for them, it granted to the new state the right to select from the public domain more than 103 million acres "which are vacant, unappropriated, and unreserved. . . ." Despite the fact that aboriginal title had never been extinguished, the state considered lands used by Alaska Natives for subsistence activities to fall within the public domain.

Attempts to regulate Native subsistence activities began in earnest after 1958. They met stiff resistance from the Natives. For example, in 1961, federal agents arrested two Inupiat hunters at Barrow for hunting migratory waterfowl out of season in contravention of migratory bird treaties to which the United States is signatory. The rights of the Inupiat to take birds had never been challenged in the past, despite the treaties which closed the bird-hunting season between March 10 and September 1, effectively eliminating the possibility of hunting migratory game birds in the Arctic. Nearly 140 Inupiat hunters went out and shot eider ducks, then presented themselves and their evidence to the local magistrate. The charges against the two hunters who had been arrested were dropped.

By this time, Native people throughout the state had come to understand what the Indians of southeast Alaska had known since the turn of the century. As Austin Hammond, chief of the Tlingit Indians' Sockeye Clan, testified, "the arrival of White people is like a tidal wave—they come in and are pounding on your shores."

By 1966, Alaska Natives had established a statewide organization, the Alaska Federation of Natives. At the federation's first convention, it recommended that the Department of the Interior should freeze all disposals of federal land pending a land claims settlement, that Congress should pass a law to settle land claims, and that Alaska Natives should be consulted before the passage of any such law. Secretary of the Interior Stewart Udall did freeze the conveyance of state-selected lands in 1966, an action that gave impetus to the idea that Alaska Natives had claims that must be settled soon.

The judgment obtained by the Tlingit and Haida in 1968, more than thirty years after their suit was begun, was plainly an inadequate model. The judgment was, moreover, only for monetary compensation: it did not return any land to the Natives. The idea that a legislated settlement of Native claims was preferable to the uncertainties of litigation began to take hold in Alaska.

After the discovery in 1968 of oil at Prudhoe Bay, the oil companies aligned themselves with proponents of a legislated settlement because of the likelihood that litigation by the Natives might hold up indefinitely the granting of a right of way for the construction of a nine-hundred-mile pipeline from Prudhoe Bay to the Gulf of Alaska. Besides, an increasing number of persons believed that Congress had a moral obligation to settle Native claims. Legislators in Alaska and in Washington, D.C., recognized that the question of aboriginal claims in Alaska could be postponed no longer.

The Settlement

With the passage of ANCSA in 1971, Congress extinguished by legislation the aboriginal title Alaska Natives held to their lands throughout Alaska, and it extinguished also their aboriginal right to hunt and fish on these lands. The Natives would receive title to forty-four million acres of land, about ten percent of Alaska's territory. After the passage of ANCSA and the Alaska National Interest Lands Act (ANILCA) in 1980, the federal government had reserved for itself 197 million acres of land, about sixty percent of the state. The State of Alaska was allowed to select 124 million acres, about thirty percent of the state. In compensation for the 321 million acres of land, ninety percent of the state, that the federal and state governments had appropriated, ANCSA provided for the payment to Alaska Natives of $962.5 million, about three dollars per acre.

ANCSA required the establishment of twelve regional corporations and more than two hundred village corporations. Most Natives enrolled both in their local village corporation and in the regional corporation established for the region in which the village was located. The typical village shareholder holds one hundred shares in the village corporation and one hundred shares in the regional corporation. Natives who do not live in a village but are nevertheless identified with a region became stockholders only in a regional corporation: they are known as at-large stockholders. Natives who did not permanently reside in the state were allowed to join one of the twelve regional corporations or a thirteenth regional corporation, which is based in Seattle. The 13th Regional Corporation (its official name) received no land, but it did receive a *pro rata* share of the $962.5 million. In total, some eighty thousand Native persons who claimed to have at least one-quarter Native blood became either village or at-large shareholders. There was only one issue of shares. No one born after December 18, 1971, the date on which Congress passed ANCSA, received shares.

Village corporations received title to twenty-two million of the forty-four million acres that under ANCSA were to be conveyed to the Natives. Six of the regional corporations divided among themselves sixteen million acres on a formula that was intended to apportion large land claims among the disproportionately small populations of these regions. The other six regional corporations received small acreages out of two million acres set aside for special purposes. Five former reservations, which had chosen to be excluded from most of ANCSA's other provisions, established village corporations, which received title to the surface and subsurface estate of their reservations, totalling about four million acres.

The village corporations received only surface title to their lands. The regional corporations received the subsurface title to the village lands within their region, as well as surface and subsurface title to the land they received independently of village selections.

ANCSA gave villages the option of incorporating as a profit-making or a non-profit-making corporation, but they were advised that, under Alaska law, there could be no distribution of dividends to members of a non-profit corporation. All of the villages chose to establish profit-making corporations; indeed, they were expected to make this choice as the best way to enter a brave new world of commercial enterprise and prosperity.

To balance regional disparities in natural resources, ANCSA required each regional corporation to distribute seventy percent of its annual revenues from the sale of timber and mineral resources among the twelve regional corporations on a per capita basis. Within each region, these receipts are divided equally between the regional corporation on the one hand and the village corporations and at-large shareholders on the other.

This simple recital of ANCSA's main provisions gives some idea of the act's complexity: it is difficult for anyone to grasp all of its implications at once.

Of the $962.5 million compensation, Congress agreed to provide $462.5 million through annual appropriations over an eleven-year period. A revenue-sharing scheme for the mineral reve-

nues (including oil) from both federal and state lands provided
the remaining $500 million. All of these monies were deposited
in the Alaska Native Fund, established by the U.S. Treasury.
The Treasury disbursed these funds on an annual basis to the
regional corporations and, through them, to the village corporations and individuals. These payments were completed in 1981.

Several Native organizations established during the 1960s as
anti-poverty, community-development agencies supported
ANCSA and, except for the Arctic Slope Native Association,
agreed to it. Although the Alaska Natives who led these several
organizations realized that ANCSA was defective on many
counts, they nevertheless felt it was the best deal they could get
at the time. A fortuitous combination of economic and political
events had provided them with an opportunity these leaders
believed was unlikely to occur again. Today, however, in the
villages, Alaska Natives complain that they were not consulted:
there were no hearings and no vote on ANCSA in the villages.
Lillian Liliabas of Akiak asked:

Who voted for ANCSA? Raise your hands! You see, Mr. Berger,
no hands! You won't find 10 people on the Kuskokwim who voted
for ANCSA!

Having relinquished aboriginal title to and aboriginal rights
in the whole state, Alaska Natives confidently expected that
their ownership of the forty-four million acres that ANCSA had
conveyed to them would be secure and their way of life protected. This expectation is precisely what ANCSA has not
achieved. ANCSA offered no guarantee in perpetuity of Native
ownership of land nor did it protect Native subsistence. Millie
Buck, speaking at Gulkana, concluded, "It is no settlement as
long as we have to worry about losing our land."

The Problems of the Settlement

Native leaders became the executives of the newly established
Native corporations. These Native corporate executives, the
managers of Native businesses and Native investments, have

given Alaska Natives political influence, because of their new economic power, that they did not have before. As Roger Lang of Juneau declared, "We have become a fairly significant political force and . . . we own a bank, we do several things not even dreamt of ten to fifteen years [ago]. We're also finding out that you can be a Native banker and a Native lawyer and a Native teacher."

A new world beckoned, but only a relatively few could enter it. The promise of ANCSA has not been fulfilled. It has become, instead, a symbol of failed expectations, the focus of every discontent. Martin Moore was the first of 1,450 witnesses who testified at the hearings I held. He is a resident of Emmonak and secretary of Calista Corporation, the Native regional corporation. He said:

> The land claims settlement act raises a lot of questions. The people here, if you talk to them on a person-to-person basis, will testify and tell you that they really haven't gained anything as far as livelihood and welfare of the people are concerned. The claims settlement act, to this date, has never put any food on the table yet. You could ask these people sitting here. They're still living the same way they lived centuries and thousands of years ago. They don't have jobs. They don't have checks from the regional corporations. They're still the same.

What had seemed like an enormous sum of money, nearly a billion dollars, turned out to be quite a modest sum, once it was distributed among all the corporations and their shareholders. Construction of the trans-Alaska pipeline after ANCSA's passage accelerated in Alaska a period of national inflation: the purchasing power of the dollar had decreased by about one-third by the time the corporations received their money. On a state-wide basis, ANCSA's cash settlement amounted to about $12,-000 for each shareholder, but individual Natives did not receive this sum. The at-large shareholders, who do not live in the villages, each received $6,525. Most village shareholders received a total of $375; but after 1976, the Alaska Native Fund made no further payments to villagers.

There can be no doubt that the amount of ANCSA's cash

compensation caught the public's eye. Millie Buck, speaking at Gulkana, remarked that constant reiteration of the generosity of the settlement had left White people with the idea that an Indian who was driving a new car had not worked for it but had simply bought it from a share of the settlement. Lena Dewey, at Nenana, said, "You have a lot of the White community against anything that's Native because of the land claims, because they thought we got so much." Jack Oktollik of Kotzebue commented:

> Ever since I went out of state in Oregon, every White man I see say, "Hey, a rich man." I said, "No, I am not rich. Just because I am from Alaska . . . doesn't mean that I am rich. I had to make a living like everybody else."

The Native corporations were created by a reversal of the usual process whereby some individuals notice an economic opportunity, then organize to exploit it by forming a corporation and looking for capital. The Native corporations were not formed to meet a particular need in an established market. ANCSA required Natives to organize corporations, provided them with capital, then urged them to find or create economic opportunities. They had to formulate their business purposes after the fact. Nor were the Native shareholders investors in the sense that Wall Street understands the word. They were not a random group of shareholders, but a people bound together by land, culture, and kinship ties. Louis Jones, at Ketchikan, pointed out that the shareholders would not ordinarily have had any money to invest, yet each shareholder is considered to have invested $12,000 in the Native corporations in 1971. "Very, very few would have put that into stocks," said Jones. The idea that Alaska Natives are shareholders is an artificial concept.

For a great many of these so-called investors, receipt of income from this investment, negligible though it may be, threatened their eligibility for welfare programs. To ensure that payments received from the Alaska Native Fund would not make Natives ineligible for food stamps and other benefits, Congress declared in 1976 that ANCSA payments "constitute compensation for the extinguishment of claims to land, and shall not be deemed to substitute for any governmental programs otherwise available to the Native people of Alaska as citizens of the United States and the State of Alaska." Dividends, however, are another matter. Judy Bush, a Legal Services lawyer who testified at Fairbanks, discussed the situation of elderly and disabled Natives on fixed incomes. When they receive dividends, "then their benefits from the government are cut back."

The artificial nature of the Native corporations confounds their purposes and functions; directors need not declare dividends in order to attract and keep shareholders; shareholders are assigned to them by an act of Congress; shares cannot be sold or traded for twenty years; if, through inheritance, non-Natives receive stock, they cannot vote it until 1992. If one of the twelve regional corporations sells timber or receives income from subsurface minerals, it must share seventy percent of the revenue among all twelve regions; corporations that are losing money on their own operations must nevertheless share their revenues.

The regional corporations are far from eager to share seventy percent of their revenue from the sale of natural resources. If such an investment fails, the corporation must bear the whole loss; if it succeeds, more than two-thirds of the profit must be shared with other regional corporations.

Because of this confusion, some commentators have wondered whether Native corporations should be treated as corporations, civic entities, or fiduciary institutions. Native people wonder, too.

The Native people themselves are often under a misapprehension regarding the land—they think it is their land, when it is in fact corporate land.

If you own stock in General Motors, you can't walk in there and drive off in one of their cars. It is the same thing with us; we can't walk over here and put up a house on our land or something. That is a big fallacy, or whatever you want to call it, that a lot of people perceive that we own the land. What it is is that our corporation owns the land. Sure, we elect the board of directors. I sit on the board of directors myself. However, there is certain things that you have to follow in a profitable corporation, and a lot of those rules of the game don't allow you to get involved into the social, political aspects of the Native people that the Native peoples so much expect from a corporation. *(Don Standifer, Tyonek)*

Few Alaska Natives in 1971 had any training or experience in the management of business enterprises. The advice they received was often bad. Mistakes were made, some of them costly. Because of the conflicts inherent in ANCSA, the early years of implementing it were characterized by misunderstanding and strife. Officers of the corporations had to devote inordinate amounts of time, energy, and money to negotiation, litigation, administrative appeals, and lobbying. Delays in the conveyance of land to the corporations severely handicapped their planning and development.

Janie Leask, president of Alaska Federation of Natives, Inc., said in a submission made in 1984 to the President's Commission on Indian Reservation Economies:

> What has fallen on Native people and their institutions during the past thirteen years is a legal and administrative burden so overwhelming that in many ways implementing ANCSA has become an end itself. . . .
>
> The entire effort has drawn off tens of millions of dollars which more properly could have been put into business investments, human-resource development, communication between stockholders and corporate leaders, and training and technical assistance for village corporation personnel.
>
> If the implementation costs were heavy for the regions, it was worse for the villages, especially for the small ones, because they had so little cash from the Alaska Native Fund to begin with. We now have villages which are almost broke from going through the steps of incorporation, corporate elections, enrollments, stock issuances, land selections, land conveyances, CPA audits, meetings, decisions, public reporting, etc., etc., etc. They haven't made much money or really engaged in much economic development activity. *But they have implemented ANCSA.* And many of them have now come to a point where they may have to sell some of their land in order to keep going. [Emphasis in original]

ANCSA provided that "the settlement should be accomplished rapidly . . . without litigation," but now this exhortation

echoes across a legal landscape littered with the debris of innu-
merable lawsuits. Tens of millions of dollars have been spent on
the litigation of these disputes. Disputes have covered a whole
range of matters that include the delineation of land-selection
boundaries between regions; eligibility of villages for certifica-
tion as village corporations; shares of revenue from the sale of
timber and mineral resources; and, of course, proxy battles
within the corporations themselves. The people of Kodiak com-
plained of a debilitating lawsuit between the village corporations
and the regional corporation. Superior Court Judge Roy
Madsen, himself an Alaska Native from Kodiak, said:

> We've seen numerous lawsuits that have sprung up because of
> technicalities in the proxies. This has placed a financial burden on
> the village corporations. In fact, [it] has broken some, and the
> people that are elected to serve the rest of the people in the villages
> are subjected to threats of lawsuits or actually have been sued, and
> it just compounds the financial burden all the way around.

As Marvin Frost of Afognak put it:

> Litigation has hurt this region, perhaps it will bankrupt this region
> and many of the villages. . . . Millions of dollars was spent.

The complaint is reiterated in every region.

More than anything else, ANCSA has divided Alaska Natives.
Mike Gaffney, professor of Native studies at the University of
Alaska, Fairbanks, observed that conflict has become institu-
tionalized among Alaska Natives. Villages and subsistence
against region and profit, village shareholders against at-large
shareholders, urban shareholders against village shareholders,
urban corporations against village corporations.

> The first result of the settlement act was to separate all the people
> that used to be together. Everybody became distinct different vil-
> lages. Regions became different regions. Some regions even split
> in half just so that they would get their own control. That was the
> first indication of what was to come. Boundaries were fought over,
> whereas two groups of Natives or two villages, who never had a
> problem before, they start fighting over the boundaries. There were

a lot of special ramifications of what happened and nobody stopped to think. *(Jack Wick, Larsen Bay)*

ANCSA has made its scars on Gambell today . . . the scars that I am talking about were the dividing up the people . . . and that is a big scar to the community itself—to the people—because we think . . . out here we think as one, work as one and live as one. *(Branson Tungiyan, Gambell)*

Conflicts have occurred between village and regional corporations over whether or not resources should be classified as surface or subsurface resources. Gravel is often the only resource of commercial value on village corporation land, and the question of its being a surface or subsurface resource has been litigated for years. It still remains unsettled. Kathy Grimness of Unalaska said, "We can't even get our own gravel off our own land."

Some communities were excluded from ANCSA. Ketchikan, Wrangell, Petersburg, Haines, and Seward received no land at all, because their Native populations were less than half of these towns' total population. Yet Juneau, Sitka, Kenai, and Kodiak were permitted to form corporations, even though none of them has a fifty percent Native population. These four towns became urban corporations, and each of them was permitted to select land. Because there was no land available near them, their selections had to be made some distance away, sometimes encompassing traditional lands of other villages. As a result, there have been conflicts between urban and village corporations. Shee Atika, Sitka's urban corporation, wishes to engage in logging on land it holds at Cube Cove on Admiralty Island. The people of Angoon living on the island oppose this activity because they use this land for subsistence.

Some village shareholders live in distant cities. Some non-Natives have acquired shares by inheritance. Shareholders who are not closely connected to the village may, in time, dominate the boards of village corporations, with the result that local concerns may be neglected or voted down. Such conflicts usually center on development activities or the payment of dividends, and they would not be surprising if they occurred in a normal corporate context. In the cultural context of village Alaska, however, they create divisions that may imperil the protection of village lands and subsistence activities.

Village Corporations

Larry Merculieff, president of the St. Paul Island village corporation, cited the "host of obstacles" in the path of village corporations:

> Little seed capital, lack of local business opportunities, lack of infrastructure adequate for business development in the community, lack of human resources trained and/or experienced in the business arena, the leadership spread too thin by the numerous demands placed on them from inside the village and out, political pressures to invest in something despite odds of succeeding or risk, the bias of the business community, internal and external conflicts brought about by ANCSA's ambiguities and unrealistic shareholder expectations.

A village corporation with one hundred shareholders received about $80,000 from the initial distribution of funds in December 1973. The Alaska Native Foundation has calculated that the minimum cost to a village of carrying out the corporate duties that ANCSA has imposed on it is about $70,000 annually. Over ten years, most villages received less than $200,000 in total from the Native Fund, and that amount could not long support operating budgets, let alone pay dividends. As early as 1974, a study carried out by the Department of the Interior estimated that any village with fewer than six hundred shareholders had little chance of success. Only eight villages out of the more than two hundred village corporations exceeded six hundred shareholders; another five had five hundred or more shareholders. From the beginning, the great majority of village corporations were seriously undercapitalized.

Now some village corporations are obliged to sell land to hire lawyers and accountants to keep them in good standing under state corporate law. Others have simply stopped filing reports required by the state. As a result, there is very little reliable information about the financial condition of the village corporations. According to Glenn Fredericks, president of Kuskokwim Corporation, who testified at Bethel, many village corporations are now without funds. They are failing, and "creditors will be out there attaching the land."

The first task of the newly formed village corporations was to select their lands, and they usually chose land for subsistence, rather than land that had possibilities for economic development. Then they had to reconvey title to plots used for residences and business sites. But ANCSA also required them to reconvey up to 1,280 acres to the state-chartered local government or in trust to the state where no local government has been set up. They have usually been obliged to employ staff or consultants (or both) to obtain conveyance of the lands selected and to arrange for these reconveyances. The acreage to be reconveyed to the local government is often the only commercially valuable land owned by the corporation. Village corporations have been forced to spend their modest wealth in making their land selections, litigating to secure their land conveyances, and implementing the surrender of the only land they have that has commercial value.

Much of the land held by village corporations is tundra, without any commercial possibilities. Whatever may be done to change Alaska Natives, we cannot change the climate, geography, or economic prospects of their villages. In the Lower 48, development followed a pattern: clearing the forest, the rise of agriculture, establishment of manufacturing, the proliferation of cities as centers of commerce. This pattern of development cannot be applied to rural Alaska, where the possibilities for any kind of economic development are few. Many village corporations have taken over the local store and fuel station; often they are the only business opportunities in town.

This year more people are working and have an idea of raising money, but we do not know a whole lot about economic development ventures. We are being pressured, whether we want to or not, to raise money in order to keep our corporations operating. *(Muffy Iya, Savoonga)*

Sanak Island; there's not anything out there any more and actually I don't think the land is worth anything. There's only 26 [shareholders]. . . . There is no business. All the money we make is on the grazing lease that we graze it out every year. That's all the money we make on it. We've been getting $5,000 a year. *(Chris Gunderson, Sand Point)*

Some village corporations that have no surface assets or business opportunities have banked their capital; they may be profitable, although inactive. Others have no business to carry on and they have little capital left; they do nothing more than comply with formal statutory requirements. Larry Evanoff of Chenega Bay said of his village corporation, which has only sixty-nine shareholders, "We pay our taxes, we pay for our audits, and that's about it." Others have ceased even to do this much.

Whereas many village corporations function only on paper, a few villages in southeast Alaska hold substantial tracts of timber, and some village corporations in south-central Alaska have land that has become valuable because of its proximity to Anchorage. For example, the village corporation at Kassan in southeast Alaska, which has approximately a hundred shareholders, sold some of its timber in 1979. It paid each shareholder $25,000 and invested the balance to provide, out of interest, an annual dividend of $10,000 to each shareholder. Village corporations that are under pressure to pay dividends may sell off valuable assets to do so. Klukwan, Inc. is selling some of its timber to make distributions to shareholders. According to Ed Warren, a member of the Klukwan board, dividends through profits are "a generation away."

In addition to the problems already described, there are many other impediments to the success of village corporations. Larry Merculieff, president of the St. Paul village corporation, described the larger burden:

Like all village corporations, we face the widespread negative image . . . towards Native corporations; of being viewed as politically volatile, unstable in management, and having business naiveté and ignorance. It is this view . . . albeit justified, that makes it difficult, if not impossible, for most village corporations to leverage what little capital they have or to have reputable and successful business partners. Lack of financing or of good business partners often result in village corporations going totally on their own or getting into bed with scheming business partners. Either way, the odds of profitability are quite slim, and losses and bad mistakes highly likely. I would assume you have found that the majority of village corporations are either doing nothing or failing badly.

Wassie Balluta, president of Nondalton village corporation in the Bristol Bay region, explained that "People come along, talk the board of directors into things—sweet deals. Next thing you know, you're flat on your back."

Few Natives living in village Alaska in 1971 had any business experience. Moreover, village leaders, including corporate officers, are usually away from the village during the peak periods of subsistence activities. For a variety of good reasons, few village corporations have been successful—but not because they are Native corporations. In most villages, no commercial business could have succeeded, and the bankruptcy of many village corporations seems to be inevitable. In this event, the corporation's land, in many cases its only asset, can be seized by creditors. Under ANCSA, villagers were forced to place all of their ancestral lands in the corporation. All of their land is now at risk. Vulnerability was built into this scheme.

> The corporate structure has been set up for a person to put whatever amount of wealth that he wishes to put into that corporation. But, no, not the Alaska Native. The Alaska Native put everything, the land, the money and, according to the ANCSA, they put their birthright and everything else into that corporate structure that we hate so much. *(Walter Johnson, Anchorage)*

> Nobody in their right mind, in America, would take all of their assets and put them into a business and go one hundred percent, which we were forced to do as Native groups. *(Sid Casey, Seattle)*

Regional Corporations

ANCSA's successes and failures have been judged largely by the performance of the regional corporations. The media have given extensive coverage to stories about losses, the possibilities of bankruptcy, and conflicts with village corporations that might have gone unnoticed had they been about ordinary corporations. Shareholders have often regarded the regional corporations as governmental institutions and expected them to engage in political activities of one sort or another and to deliver social services. Above all, stockholders have expected the regional corporations to protect traditional ways of life and ancestral lands used for subsistence. During the referendum on subsistence in 1982, regional corporations were instrumental in securing a statewide affirmation of the priority subsistence should take over other uses of the land. At the same time, shareholders expect the corporations to be profitable, to provide employment, and to pay regular dividends. The corporations quickly found that, if they are to make a profit, they must participate in the principal activities of Alaska's economy. Even then, they may fail to serve their shareholders' aspirations. Village corporations experience the same discrepancy between subjective expectations and objective reality, but the dilemma is felt more keenly at the regional level. In the early days, shareholders and managers alike held idealistic dreams for the future, but they have given way to realistic strategies for corporate survival. Byron Mallott, president of Sealaska Corporation, spoke of the

> overwhelming reality of what it takes to make a business corporation work. It is an all-consuming effort. It requires the kind of focus on business that virtually precludes a focus on other things that really are important. Because if for one minute you take your mind off the business, all sorts of things begin to go awry because your competitors aren't doing the same thing.

In theory, the regional corporations can provide shareholders with jobs and pay them dividends, but in fact they have employed only a few shareholders, and most corporations have never paid regular dividends. Sealaska, the largest of the regional corporations, has never paid a dividend. On this point, Charlie Johnson, president of Bering Straits Native Corporation and chairman of the Alaska Federation of Natives, Inc., remarked, "You know the benefits of the land claims act really have fallen to only a few. And that few are those of us that are employed by the corporations. The primary economic benefit has been to those that have been employed by the corporations, and it has not fallen to the general Native population."

More information is available on the financial condition of the regional corporations than for the village corporations. According to the *ANCSA 1985 Study,* prepared for the Secretary of the Interior and known as the 1985 study:

> At the regional level, only one corporation has not reported a loss since its formation—and more than one has had to consider bankruptcy. In recent years, the regional corporations have been able to devote more of their concern to long-term issues of corporate management. For many, general and administrative expenses are declining as a portion of total assets and net income. Long-term debt is modest. Natural resource income is beginning to appear and show significant growth. Certain corporations are investing in rural Alaska with at least some success. The regional corporations' combined net income continues to be modest, however, and losses are commonplace.

These losses can be significant: in 1982, Sealaska lost $28 million; in 1983, Doyon, Ltd. lost $21 million. Bering Straits Native Corporation has been teetering on the verge of bankruptcy for almost a decade.

There have been successes. Ahtna, Inc., the smallest of the regional corporations, has always shown a profit. Roy Ewan, its president, speaking at Copper Center, explained that

> We have in this area quite a few people working on the pipeline and we have a person working in the State, and we have our construction company. . . . We have CRNA, which is Copper River Native Association, which employs quite a few people. Certainly I think this was a big plus. Maybe it hasn't come about just because of land claims, but it had a lot to do with it.

Cook Inlet Region, Inc. and Ahtna, Inc. are the only regional corporations whose shareholders' equity is significantly higher in value than it was in 1981.

In general, the financial condition and prospects of the regional corporations are considered to be healthier than those of the village corporations. The regional corporations received sufficient capital. They employed the Natives who had the most experience in the dominant society, they could afford to employ professional assistance, and they now have a decade of experience behind them.

Regional corporations have invested in stocks and bonds, construction, resource development, hotel management, real estate, food processing, tourism, and pipeline maintenance companies. These investments are not, in general, in rural Alaska, and they do not provide much employment for shareholders in the villages. Sometimes a regional corporation can provide employment by taking over existing businesses, but few new jobs are thereby created.

In 1984, the Alaska Department of Labor studied the effects that regional corporations have had on the state's economy. It found that regional corporations annually employ an average of 1,800 persons, Native and non-Native. More than half this number are employed in the Anchorage area, most of them in corporation-owned hotels. On the other hand, the regional corporations employ only forty-five persons in southwest Alaska where the population is predominantly Native. Only Cook Inlet Region, Inc. has broken down its employment figures: of forty-six persons the corporation directly employs, twenty-one are Native. No figures are given for the corporation's subsidiaries but, according to the study, "The greater percent are non-Native due to the inflexibility of union call-out procedures." The employees of the regional corporations, it seems clear, are predominantly non-Native. Only fifteen percent of Sealaska's employees is Native; it would be surprising if the average figure for the other regional corporations was higher.

An entire industry has sprung up in Alaska to administer Native corporations; professional staff is required, not only to run the business but also to select land, to keep track of shareholders' ever-fragmenting interests, to prepare annual reports and proxy statements, to keep accounts, and to fulfill ANCSA's seemingly endless requirements. Few Natives have the formal qualifications required for these jobs, so they usually go to non-Natives. As the 1985 study says:

ANCSA played a part in increasing employment of Natives in the private sector, although the specific number of jobs provided to Natives by ANCSA corporations is undetermined. Survey data show that a minority of Natives have worked for a Native corporation. There has been improvement in employment for Alaska Natives since passage of ANCSA, but ANCSA's role in that improvement was minor in comparison to the role of government. ANCSA has not, by itself, enabled Natives "to compete with non-Natives and to raise their standard of living through their own efforts."

In the end, the benefits that regional corporations confer on Alaska Natives are likely to be minimal. Corporate success is measured in terms that are irrelevant to the shareholders in the villages. A healthy balance sheet cannot always be translated into jobs or dividends; it may only mean that the corporation is carrying on business at a profit with predominantly non-Native employees. Even where profits are made, the shares are so widely held that the income to each shareholder is very likely to be insignificant. Nevertheless, the possibility of a regional corporation's bankruptcy is of great concern to the villages within the region because the regional corporations hold title to the subsurface of village lands.

Have regional corporations contributed to Alaska's economy? The state's principal industry, the exploration and development of oil and gas reserves, requires huge amounts of capital and professional technical experience. Some regional corporations have entered this field, usually by the leasing of oil-bearing acreage to oil companies. There have been few joint ventures because the corporations do not have enough capital and lack technical competence. Even limited participation in oil ventures has brought them into conflict with their own villages, whose primary concern is the preservation of habitat for fish and wildlife.

Tension over conflicting views of land use appeared early in ANCSA's history. In 1976, when I was holding hearings in Canada on the proposed Mackenzie Valley gas pipeline, Mayor Eben Hopson, of the predominantly Inupiat North Slope Borough and founder of the Inuit Circumpolar Conference, submitted a statement on the Inupiat experience with oil and gas development on the North Slope.

The politics of oil have had a very divisive influence in rural Alaska. . . . Many of [the Alaska Native] regional corporations have signed exploration and option agreements with oil corporations, and several of these regional corporations have begun to appear to be politically aligned with their oil corporate partners.

This tendency to assist the oil corporations avoid taxes may extend even to the point that our regional Native corporations will oppose the development of home-rule government in rural Alaska. Rather than fight for local self-determination for our people, the influence of the oil corporations may lead our regional corporations to fight against it. Even now, in fact, I wonder if we could have organized the North Slope Borough today against the opposition of my own Arctic Slope Regional Corporation, of which I am a vice-president. I worry about the direction that the politics of oil is taking among our people in the Arctic.

In 1979, NANA Regional Corporation joined with oil interests to bid on leases in the Beaufort Sea, a sale that the North Slope Borough and several Native villages were opposing in court. These conflicts continue. In 1984, the Native villages of Stebbins and Gambell sued to enjoin Norton Sound offshore drilling in which Calista Corporation is a partner. At Anaktuvuk Pass, shareholders in Arctic Slope Regional Corporation resent an exchange of land the corporation has made with the federal government. To obtain oil-bearing land on the Arctic coast, the corporation gave up land it owned that offered the villagers at Anaktuvuk Pass unimpeded access to caribou on federal lands. Now this land is under federal jurisdiction and village access to caribou has been restricted.

During the early days of ANCSA, Professor Monroe Price wrote:

In a sense, the gospel of capitalism has gripped the leadership of the regional corporations just as in another day, another kind of gospel was introduced for its educative and assimilative influence. The profitmaking mandate has become a powerful vision, a powerful driving force.

The corporate executives will be those who are willing to forego subsistence activities, to place a higher priority on board meetings than on salmon fishing, and to spend time talking to lawyers and financiers and bankers rather than the people of the villages. It is possible that there will develop a leadership cadre in the Native corporations that will become somewhat removed from the shareholders. The Native corporations, in this sense, will approximate other large businesses and that management will, more and more, be separated from ownership.

To the extent that this has happened, it represents the fulfillment of the expectations Congress had. It also means that corporate executives in the urban centers may be estranged from their shareholders in the villages.

Economic Effects

ANCSA's greatest claim to success, a claim advanced by Roy Huhndorf, president of Cook Inlet Region, Inc., is that the hundreds of millions of dollars the corporations received have contributed to the development of the Alaskan economy. Mr. Huhndorf explains:

First, what has occurred in the period following 1971 is the transfer of forty-four million acres out of government hands into private ownership. Prior to 1971 less than one percent of Alaska's land was in private ownership. When land conveyances have been completed to the Native corporations, approximately twelve percent of Alaska's land will be in private hands.

From the perspective of resource development, this was a particularly important change. The marketplace of opportunity for mineral development, timber, oil and gas development, and for other uses, has changed tremendously as a consequence. Evidence of this is the quantity of land that Native corporations have been able to commit for development over the past ten years.

Development agreements on Native lands have . . . caused more than $750 million to be spent on exploration and development activities over the past six years. The Native corporations have recognized that their destiny is tightly bound to Alaska and, as a consequence, they have taken an interest in the basic industries of the state, industries that are important for the economic health of the Native community and the state as a whole. Commercial fishing, cannery operations, air travel, construction, oil and gas, minerals, coal, timber, and industry-support service businesses have all benefited from substantial investments from Native corporations.

The ANCSA money, nearly a billion dollars, compensation for extinguishment of aboriginal title, was not paid directly to Alaska Natives nor was it expended directly for their benefit. The economic benefits of ANCSA have been greater for non-Natives than for Natives.

It is true that in the past decade, health, housing, and education in village Alaska have improved, not because of ANCSA, however, but because of increased federal and state spending. Janie Leask, president of Alaska Federation of Natives, Inc., comments on this point in her submission to the President's Commission on Indian Reservation Economies:

> Most of the enormous flow of public works, services and jobs to the bush during the past fifteen years has come from Prudhoe Bay (through the appropriations process of state government) and from federal human service programs. It has been public capital, not ANCSA land and money, which accounts for the changes. . . . ANCSA has brought little or no direct benefit to the Native family. The average corporate stockholder has received no land and only a few hundred dollars in mandatory distributions from the Alaska Native Fund. Some corporations, primarily regions, have declared dividends of a dollar or two per share. But when one compares this with the tens of millions of dollars which have flowed to the villages from state and federal treasuries, there is no question as to where the causes of the general improvement lie.

Despite ANCSA and its millions, Native people who had little money before 1971 have little money today. If they have more now, it is not because of ANCSA. Where there was unemployment, there is still no work. Where unemployment has been alleviated, it is not because of ANCSA.

Defenders of ANCSA argue that the corporations it established have been going through a period of learning. Having learned from experience, the corporations, they say, will soon be making substantial profits and paying dividends to their shareholders. This prospect seems unlikely. The 1985 study, prepared for the Secretary of the Interior, asserts that:

> Resource development in Alaska has remained at a low level—due primarily to the economic environment rather than to lack of knowledge about the resource base. Indications are that the oil and gas industry will remain a strong and growing presence in the economy for fifty to seventy-five years, but any predictions about the timing, location, and magnitude of petroleum development are highly speculative. Due to high production and transportation costs and stiff competition from oil and natural gas, coal export expansion will be slow, and any major expansion of domestic coal markets is unlikely before the end of the century. Similarly, Alaska will see only modest expansion of nonfuel mineral development over the next decades because of high production costs and generally unfavorable Federal policies regarding domestic production. As renewable resources—fisheries, forest products, tourism—are being exploited at near-maximum levels, little growth can be expected in those industries.

Since the development of Prudhoe Bay, ninety percent of the State of Alaska's revenue has been derived from oil. Although the 1985 study refers to oil as "a strong and growing presence," in fact, state revenue from oil production is declining. There has been little other new economic development in Alaska in the past decade that is not related to oil production and to servicing the oil industry. Some say that the extension of the Cold War to the circumpolar region constitutes Alaska's best hope for continued growth. Others, I think with better cause, suggest that the state's best hope lies in the expansion of the tourist industry.

Since 1971, the government structures in Anchorage, Juneau, and Fairbanks have doubled in size, an effect of the oil boom. Two-thirds of the new jobs in rural Alaska are with government, and most of these jobs have gone to Whites, even though many of these jobs have been created to provide social services to Alaska Natives. There has been little or no expansion of the state's resource base; Alaska's major employer is and will continue to be government. Comparatively few Natives secure any of these jobs. ANCSA was based on false assumptions about the economy of village Alaska and false assumptions about the economy of Alaska as a whole.

Native corporations had been able to sustain their early losses because, until 1981, they continued to receive injections of capital from the Alaska Native Fund. Now that these annual payments have ceased, there are likely to be losses on a scale that banks, suppliers, and shareholders will not tolerate. The likelihood of failures and bankruptcies in the years before 1991, and thereafter, is greater than ever. Improved business practices are unlikely to avert these dangers, although there is no doubt that Native executives are better managers now than they were during the first decade of operations. But the weaknesses inherent in the theory of development on which ANCSA is based have not changed. The limited number and extent of economic opportunities in rural Alaska have not changed. Costs are high, markets are far away, and resources are scarce. None of these facts is going to change, and they militate against the success of most of the Native corporations, especially the village corporations.

For the villagers holding shares in these corporations, the important point is not that they will never realize the value of their stocks, it is that they are very likely to lose their land.

ANCSA and the Idea of Development

The imposition of a settlement of land claims that is based on corporate structures was an inappropriate choice, given the realities of Native life in village Alaska. The serious changes that ANCSA has introduced to Native life are becoming ever more apparent with the passage of time. ANCSA has affected everything: family relations, traditional patterns of leadership and decision making, customs of sharing, subsistence activities, the entire Native way of life. The village has lost its political and social autonomy.

The concepts central to ANCSA emerged during the 1960s. The act itself was based on a report by the Federal Field Committee for Development Planning in Alaska, which considered Alaska Natives to have a culture of poverty and did not take into account the strengths of Native culture, economy, and government. ANCSA is a domestic application of theories of economic development that had been applied to the Third World. The premises of the foreign-aid programs greatly affected consideration of the problems to be found among the Native peoples at home. The central thesis is that, with large-scale economic development, the modern sector of the economy will expand to incorporate persons still active in the traditional sector and, in this process, the traditional sector will gradually disappear.

In Alaska this theory of development has benefited only a few, and its danger to traditional values and the subsistence economy is now clearly recognized. Institutions at the international level, such as the World Bank, which once believed that development consisted solely in large-scale, capital-intensive projects, now realize that protection of subsistence economies is vital to the well-being of the peoples they seek to aid. Jane Jacobs argues in *Cities and the Wealth of Nations* that "development cannot be given. It has to be done. It is a process, not a collection of capital goods." With ANCSA, the village shareholders waited eagerly for a new era of development to begin. But it came only in capital expenditures by government, often in the form of inappropriate technology, beyond the means or the capacity of village people to manage or to operate without massive and continuing infusions of state or federal funding. Natives have been employed to build these new institutions and their infrastructures. There is more cash in the villages, but the specific promises of ANCSA, the promises of development, have not been and cannot be fulfilled.

ANCSA is an attempt to re-create Main Street on the tundra. The widespread complaint that comparatively few Natives are benefiting from ANCSA is true. It is unsound to say that, given more time, its beneficial effects will be more widely felt in the villages. They won't. The Native corporations are trickle-down mechanisms, but the trickle will never be greater than it is now because villagers are not in a position to make claims on the stream of income resulting from economic activity. The stream may have been increased by ANCSA, but very few of the villagers are able to get closer to it.

With ANCSA, the U.S. Congress, like the governments of

other northern nations, has tried to establish artificial economic activities for Natives in rural villages. Like most such attempts, ANCSA is failing. However, just as international views have changed, so have views at home changed. Since ANCSA, settlements of Native land claims in the Arctic and sub-Arctic have concentrated on strengthening their subsistence economies. To be sure, they have provided capital for Native people to go into business, but their emphasis, a quite deliberate one, has been on subsistence. In Canada, the James Bay and Northern Quebec Agreement, signed in 1975 with the Inuit and Cree, made extensive provision for strengthening their subsistence economies. In 1984, the government of Canada and the Eskimos of the western Arctic signed an agreement that provides for various kinds of economic development, but its emphasis is on the enhancement of Native access to fish and wildlife resources.

Perhaps development should be redefined. Consideration should be given to Native ideas of development and to strengthening the Native subsistence economy. Subsistence can be a means of development, of enabling a people to be self-sufficient, of strengthening family and community life. It entails enhancement of an existing economic mode. Now that ANCSA has failed Alaska Natives, it is not surprising that they have begun to look for new ways of strengthening the subsistence economy and the village way of life.

SUBSISTENCE

Everywhere I journeyed in Alaska, villagers were engaged in traditional subsistence activities: hunting, fishing, and gathering. Countless illustrated books and magazines have documented this ancient way of life, and it would take many more pages than I can spare here to do justice to the diversity and extent of the subsistence activities that I observed among Alaska Natives.

The photographs that appear on the following pages frame moments in the lives of Yup'ik people of southwest Alaska. The photographer, James H. Barker, has lived for many years in Bethel, the principal community in this area. Taken in 1982 and 1983, the photographs are from a portfolio commissioned by the Alaska Humanities Forum. A similar set of photographs could have been taken of Native subsistence activities in any region of Alaska. So, to accompany these photographs, I have chosen testimony taken from the hearings I held in sixty villages all over Alaska.

Subsistence to us is . . . our spiritual way of life, our culture. . . .
(*Gladys Derendoff, Huslia*)

Our way of life should not be taken lightly and discarded. (*Waldo Bodfish, Barrow*)

We have our heritage. We've got our pride. We've got to protect that along with the land because once our subsistence way of life is gone, it is gone. (*Timothy Wonhola, New Stuyahok*)

Kotlik elder Phillip Foxie mends nets in preparation for the summer salmon harvest

Us Natives, we should have the right to live out our culture, something that cannot die . . . to take away our culture would be to take away our lives, everything we knew, everything our parents knew, everything our children should know. . . . What is that billion dollars? I'd rather have my fishing and hunting rights. (*Franklin James, Jr., Ketchikan*)

This prideful feeling—that you are representing a group of people that you were born from. You were born here. We have common interests and we're bonded together by our spirituality. (*Jerry Isaac, Tanacross*)

I don't know how anybody . . . who can place the value on my Nativeness, who can place the value on my thinking, my spirituality, I don't think anybody can. Only myself, and I think each and every one of us need to remember that we are Native and that we need to value that and protect it . . . through protection of our lands and our life-style. (*Eleanor McMullen, Port Graham*)

Native people are different. . . . Our thinking is totally different. People that are non-Native don't quite understand our way of thinking and somehow, if we could close those gaps so they can better understand them, I think many good things can happen. (*Eleanor McMullen, Port Graham*)

This land is very important for me. . . . I treasure the land very much. It mean something important to me. The land is something that provides food for everyone and I'm suggesting that the land be left alone as it is, to keep on providing food for herself and for her family. (*Lucille Westlock, Emmonak*)

After fishing through a summer night at a Black River fish camp, Joseph Kaganak and daughter Alice check in by radio with family at the home village of Scammon Bay

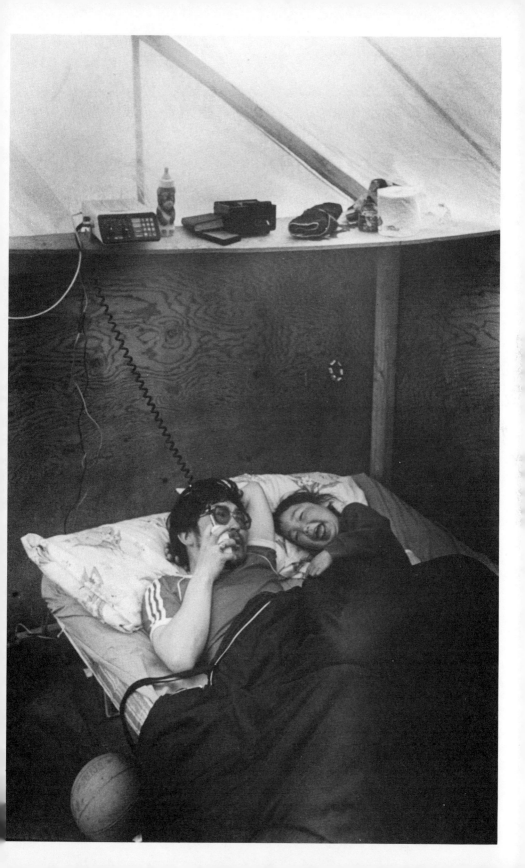

Everybody is subsistence here in the village. (*Vincent Kvasnikoff, English Bay*)

Profit to non-Natives means money. Profit to Natives means a good life derived from the land and sea, that's what we are all about, that's what this land claims was all about. Living off the land and sea is not only traditional, but owing to the scarcity of cash income, it is required for our families to survive.

. . . The land we hold in trust is our wealth. It is the only wealth we could possibly pass on to our children. Good old Mother Earth with all her bounty and rich culture we have developed from her treasures is our wealth. Without our homelands, we become true paupers. (*Antoinnette Helmer, Craig*)

We need that land to subsist, we need that land to find our food, we need that land for our children someday, so that they may use it. (*Zacharias Hugo, Anaktuvak Pass*)

These simple words of water and lands are the utmost being of us right now, giving and forming, passing on our traditional traits. (*Kenneth Nanalook, Togiak*)

God had made us, as well as the land, and gave the land to us for our use. And the land that is given to us is our clothing and our food as well as our table. (*John T. Andrew, Togiak*) [Translated by David Nanalook]

Brian, Steve, and Darryl Coffey and Alice Pete of Stebbins preserve the herring catch for winter

The land means everything to us, it brings us food, it provides for our clothing, it provides for our lodging, it brings us water; it means everything to us. (*Suzy Erlich, Kotzebue*)

One of the most important things to most people is our land. It goes back to our history and culture. That is important. As to the rest of it, who cares? (*Kurt Englestad, Seattle*)

Francis Charlie's family hauls water at Black River fish camp

Subsistence, our tradition, is very significant to our life-style. Our
people have been taught from generation to generation to respect
the land for the future generation. Knowing it's essential, the ways
have been taught from father to son. (*Leah Atakitliq, Togiak*)

*Summer sunset comes late on the tundra, drying clothes as well as
fish at Stebbins*

Helen, Maggie, and Shirley Wasuli pick berries, some to store for winter

Our roots mean our life-style. Our life-style is into the ground, the land we live on. (*Leonard Nowpakahok, Gambell*)

The land is intricately tied to our way of life. (*Homer Hunter, Scammon Bay*)

We live on this country. Many years we born, generation come generation. Everything means so much to us. Trees and grass, or rush, just everything we use. (*Margaret Escalita, Gulkana*)

We, because of the land in which we have been situated for many years, we have become a part of it. . . . (*Joe Chythlook, Aleknagik*)

In order to keep holding on to your customs and cultures, you have got to have land to get by with. If you are out of land, you are nothing. We have to belong to the land and take care of our land. (*Art Douglas, Ambler*)

The Native people have a way of life that has always been successful. . . . (*Martha Vlasloff, Tatitlek*)

This land is part of . . . our identity. The land is very important. It is part of the religion, it's part of the heritage, and to put a dollar value on it would be something that would come from Congress or from England or Switzerland or something. . . . (*Christine Smith, Fairbanks*)

George and Mona Washington collect driftwood for winter fuel

I am speaking because I am affected, and where I am affected is from the village. I remember our fathers, our forefathers, how they survived in this world, in strong winds, in cold temperatures. Many of them died during the season but they survived through thousands of years because they knew how to survive. They were taught to share, they were taught to help each others for thousands of years. Today, we are in this same situation, but this time we are not surviving against nature . . . surviving from the land. This time, we are in a time where we are searching, we are fighting to survive among different people, among different races in this Western civilization. What does this Western civilization have to offer? Business. (*Bobby Wells, Kotzebue*)

How firm we stand and plant our feet upon our land determines the strength of our children's heartbeats. (*Polly Koutchak, Unalakleet*)

We are still living and we need our land. (*Louise Wood, Shungnak*)

The way land is, it is very important and that is why it is called Mother Earth. (*Lela Omau, Nome*)

When you look through the corporate eye, our relationship to the land is altered. We draw our identity as a people from our relationship to the land and to the sea and to the resources. This is a spiritual relationship, a sacred relationship. It is in danger because, from a corporate standpoint, if we are to pursue profit and growth, and this is why profit organizations exist, we would have to assume a position of control over the land and the resources and exploit these resources to achieve economic gain. This is in conflict with our traditional relationship to the land, we were stewards, we were caretakers and where we had respect for the resources that sustained us. (*Mary Miller, Nome*)

Alan Hanson and Joseph Smith of Alakanuk prepare to place a fish trap under the thick ice

Living in this kind of culture, in this harsh environment in this part of the world, you had to have an understanding in the sense of sharing and love just to survive. (*Tom Fields, Kotzebue*)

Seal hunters from Alakanuk make the best of a bad day by fishing for tomcod

If you respect things and look at them . . . as having a spirit or being, then you're in a place where you're . . . at a balance. . . . You look at the world that way and respect it and you see that it's providing you with a way of life, and your kids. . . . (*Gabriel George, Angoon*)

Subsistence is a word that means . . . my way of life. (*Moses Toyukuk, Manokotak*)

Consider that it takes a Native to learn the real skills of hunting—this demands strength and perseverance. It takes a caring Native to pass onto the new generation the creative arts of singing and dancing. It takes a wise Native to learn the use of language—that has more meaning than words. (*John F. Moses, Emmonak*)

The great law of culture is to let one become what they were created to be. Let me be an Inupiat with the freedom to hunt, to fish, to trap, and to whale as my forefathers did in past centuries. (*Delbert Rexford, Barrow*)

We're kind of a unique people. We kind of talk to the bears, we even talk to the killer whales. . . . And it's one of those things that we respect. Because my brothers, tribal brothers are the killer whale. (*Alfred McKinley, Sr., Juneau*)

I believe that if people, if the vast majority of Alaska Natives, were given the opportunity to either kill or die for their land, that most of them would do just that if it was that simple. If you were supposed to shoot soldiers, or protect your land with firearms, there are more Natives than the federal government would like to think about that would be more than willing to do just that. The government does not operate in that clear manner anymore. Now, when they are coming in after the land and they are coming in on these issues, they come not with soldiers but with people carrying briefcases. If you shoot somebody carrying a briefcase, then you are just a criminal, not an act of war. That means that there isn't any clear way for the people to protect their land. (*Paul Ongtooguk, Kotzebue*)

Leonard Raymond hauls home his walrus catch

Launching a spring seal hunt

Clyde Smith talks with Curtis Augline, who still travels and hunts by dog team out of Alakanuk

The most important thing in the Indian life is the identity with land. . . . (*Jonathan Solomon, Fort Yukon*)

As a Native, we love our land, more than anything else. . . . the inherited land, the land we have lived on, our forefathers have left for us to govern with the knowledge of how to maintain it, with this game, with this way of care I use, therefore all of it should be passed down. (*Thomas Huneatok Brower, Barrow*)

These lands will not be separated from the people. (*Alan Panamanoff, Karluk*)

Two /

SUBSISTENCE:

MORE THAN SURVIVAL,

A WAY OF LIFE

You know, this is our farm, already developed for us. *(Wilson Sam, Huslia)*

We Inupiat are meat eaters, not vegetarians. We live off the sea mammals.
. . . The Bering Sea and the Chukchi Sea are our gardens. *(Jonah Tokienna, Wales)*

Point Hope, on the Chukchi Sea, is one of the nine whaling villages in Alaska. For thousands of years, Inupiat Eskimos have lived and taken bowhead whales here. Near the old village site, whale vertebrae encircle the graves. The Inupiat believe that these great whales give themselves to their hunters, if they have been hunted by Inupiat rules that govern the relationship between the people and the whales. Whaling crews, made up of the captain's extended family and his friends, camp near the edge of the ice, where the land-fast ice meets the open water, a line roughly parallel to the coast but often several miles offshore. On sighting a whale, they launch their umiats (wood-ribbed boats covered with bearded-seal skins stitched together by the women) and give chase. In 1984, when I was there, they caught two whales; fast-closing ice covered one, but several crews worked for two days to saw an opening through the ice to bring in their catch.

A bowhead whale may be forty feet long and weigh twenty tons. They are among the largest animals that have ever lived. Nearly the entire community will spend many hours hauling the whale up onto the ice with block and tackle, cutting up the meat and maktak (the black skin with a layer of blubber), and distributing them according to ancient rules. People spoke of this sharing:

Your hands give out to each—old people, your neighbors . . . with oil on it, with maktak on it. *(Dinah Frankson, Point Hope)*

When they catch one whale, everybody in Point Hope has a share of that maktak . . . the whale. And everybody is fed. *(Lori Kingik, Point Hope)*

I flew to Point Hope in June, at the time of the whaling festival. I saw the celebration in people's faces and heard it in their speech. Alice Solomon, at Barrow, another whaling village, described this feeling in her testimony:

The people are happy. They are smiling. They're excited, and you think about it. Boy, they caught a whale. They get really excited. And it goes all the way, the happiness extends all the way from the deep inside. And when you go into the house that caught a whale, that happiness, that excitement, that crying for joy, and remembering the deceased, because they are glad that they have been given that gift.

The whaling captains' feast, Nalukataq, lasted three days, a blend of traditional and modern ceremonies. On Sunday evening, the Episcopal church held a service of singing and thanksgiving. The choir of men and women, wearing their best parkas, sang most of the hymns in Inupiat. The women's voices were sharp and penetrating, the men's were softer. They sang in harmony. Occasionally a member of the congregation came forward to offer a profession of faith and to request a favorite hymn.

On the third day of the whaling festival, members of the two qaligi (ceremonial houses) gathered outdoors for the blanket toss. Many hands held the skin cover of an umiat like a fireman's net. Children, teenagers, and some adults then jumped high in the air on this ancient trampoline to the cheers and shouts of their friends. Dancing followed in the school gym. Male drummers sat on the floor, each holding a circular drum covered with skin. Women sat behind them and sang. First the men from one qaligi danced, one by one, sometimes in pairs; then the women. Villagers seated on the floor occasionally joined in. Later in the evening, the teenagers demonstrated their dancing, while small children ran happily around the floor, playing tag, wrestling, or imitating the serious dancers. The dancers had completed the ritual of the hunt in this triumphant reaffirmation of their way of life.

> Once a year old cultures dancing, costume wearing. Once a year for whaling. *(Dinah Frankson, Point Hope)*

Thousands of bowhead whales pass by Point Hope on the annual migration to their summer range in the Beaufort Sea. The Point Hope whalers used to take, in good years, as many as fifteen or twenty bowheads. In 1985, the International Whaling Commission limited their quota to four strikes, even if each whale that is struck escapes. One of the whaling captains asks, "How can we teach our children to be whalers if we are only permitted to take out our boats for only four strikes?" I ask myself whose rules should prevail here. The ancient laws of the Inupiat, which govern the relationship between the hunter and the whale, the distribution of the harvest, and the celebration that follows? Or the laws established by officials who live thousands of miles away? The ancient rules are enforced from within the community; outsiders impose and enforce the new laws.

> A whaling captain is faced with great responsibilities. His number-one priority is, of course, the immediate concerns of safety while out on the hazardous and icy Arctic waters. Moreover, he is [also] concerned with the sustenance of all his peoples. It is his knowledge and preparation that the people depend upon for their daily food. A whaling captain is also charged with the preservation of the great bowhead whale. This duty and responsibility of preservation of the whale has been handed down from time immemorial. *(Burton Rexford, Barrow)*

The ancient art of whaling exists alongside many examples of government-supplied amenities—the school, the state welfare office, the water truck. The people here use snowmobiles. They play basketball. They watch "Dallas" and "Donahue" on television. Like all cultures today, this one is changing too, but their ancient beliefs and values persist. The Inupiat in the whaling villages ask, "Why are we here, if not to take whales?"

We, the Inupiat people, have always shared and divided our food and that is our way of life. I do not want to lose our cultural lifestyle, because it is so precious. Our Inupiat lifestyle from time immemorial has been utilized and it is still prevalent today. We have practiced our whaling traditions and we are still using them today. . . . The whaling tradition is the most precious in my life. *(Lori Kingik, Point Hope)*

The Meaning of Subsistence

Anthropologists and lawyers have made many attempts to define subsistence, for them a technical term. For Alaska Natives, however, subsistence is a way of life.

We, the Native people, the Eskimos, we are very proud of one thing, that is our culture and our Native way of life, to live off the land, because we know culture and our tradition and way of life cannot be bought, cannot be taken away from us, no matter what happens. We live through this life, thick and thin, but that is one thing that we have, and that is, our way of life through our culture, our tradition, and the . . . words that were given to us by our forefathers and elders. Our times and what we have learned will not be taken away from us. We will hold it and try to pass it on as our elders have. *(Axel Johnson, Emmonak)*

The traditional economy is based on subsistence activities that require special skills and a complex understanding of the local environment that enables the people to live directly from the land. It also involves cultural values and attitudes: mutual respect, sharing, resourcefulness, and an understanding that is both conscious and mystical of the intricate interrelationships that link humans, animals, and the environment. To this array of activities and deeply embedded values, we attach the word "subsistence," recognizing that no one word can adequately encompass all these related concepts.

I don't know where the name subsistence came from. It's been Greek to me for a long time. But it was always understood that everybody makes a living off the land if you lived in this Yukon River valley, in this area. And you used as much land as was necessary, and you respected the other guy's trapline. . . . And everybody made a living that way. Fished during the summer, and you'd get your own fish out of it. Sell what you didn't need. Get wood in the fall. And the cycle kept on with the seasons. *(Max Huhndorf, Galena)*

When we talk about subsistence in the areas, we should be talking about Native culture and their land. I never heard the word subsistence until 1971 under the Native land claims act. Before that time, when I was brought up in the culture of my people, it's always been "our culture" and "our land." You cannot break out subsistence or the meaning of subsistence or try to identify it, and you can't break it out of the culture. The culture and the life of my Native people are the subsistence way of life. And that's what we always used, the subsistence way of life. It goes hand in hand with our own culture, our own language, and all our activities. *(Jonathon Solomon, Fort Yukon)*

Subsistence patterns follow a seasonal cycle of harvestable resources, and young hunters learn slowly and through experience the lore and skills preserved through countless generations. They accompany experienced hunters to learn by personal observation all they can about local geography, weather, animal behavior, traditional techniques of traveling, hunting, and living on the land, and how to process and preserve the products they harvest. Evelyn Higby at Point Hope noted, "They [the hunters] know where to get the eggs, they know where to find the wolves, the wolverines . . . in their area." Dinah Frankson described her uncle: "He's teaching all the . . . hunters, teaching all the tools, whaling tools, about the weather, about the currents on the sea."

Subsistence activities link the generations and the extended family into a complex network of associations, rights, and obligations. This network both reflects and re-creates the social order and gives meaning and value to each person's contributions and rewards. I have observed in village Alaska that, whether they hold office or not, leaders are men and women who provide for the needs of others in the village. Good hunters who share their harvests have always been identified as village leaders. Order in a village based on subsistence activities depends upon earned respect and consensus, not on authority and coercion.

Among the Yup'ik of Nelson Island, a young hunter brings home the first seal he kills to his mother, and she prepares to celebrate her son's first successful seal hunt. She doesn't invite everybody or her immediate relatives, she invites other mothers, one of whose daughters might make a wife for her son. In this way, a subsistence activity is used to signal a boy's achievement of manhood and to advise potential wives that he is now ready to take on new responsibilities.

Subsistence activities link the Native peoples with the animals and the land on which they all depend. Many Alaska Natives believe that spiritual ties bind their own success in hunting to the welfare of the animals on which they depend. The Koyukon Athabascans of interior Alaska extend their policy of reciprocity beyond their own kin to the wolves, by leaving a portion of their harvest for the wolves. This is done because the Koyukon believe that the wolves kill animals and leave them for the Koyukon.

Subsistence links the village in many ways with its past, it informs the present, and it is the means whereby the village can survive in the future. The land, of course, provides the resources and remoteness on which this way of life depends.

I came from a subsistence family, I grew up that way. I am very proud of it. I want my children to grow up that way. I want my great-great-great grandchildren to grow up that way and be proud of it because it brings strength to us as Inupiats. It is something different than going to AC [Alaska Commercial store], or Hansen's. Our grocery store is millions of acres wide, not just a few thousand feet, and it brings us pride. *(Suzy Erlich, Kotzebue)*

No matter what the weather may be like, to know that we own land gave us comfort, gave us refuge. It was home. From it, we gained food. From it, we gained medicine. On it, we performed the ancient ceremonies. It gave strength to the clan, it gave strength to the family life, and courage and pride to carry on their way of life. And strange as it may seem that, in 1984, that kind of thought still prevails, and it surprises me that the culture is not extinct, like in Egypt or in other parts of the world. It is very much alive. *(Walter Soboleff, Tenakee)*

Even Natives who live in cities and are not engaged in full-time subsistence activities regard subsistence as essential to their future well-being. Nelson Frank of Sitka said:

Subsistence living, a marginal way of life to most, has no such connotation to the Native people of southeast Alaska. The relationship between the Native population and the resources of the land and the sea is so close that an entire culture is reflected.

The traditional law . . . was passed from generation to generation, intact, through the repetition of legends and observance of ceremonials which were largely concerned with the use of land, water, and the resources contained therein. Subsistence living was not only a way of life, but also a life-enriching process. Conservation and perpetuation of subsistence resources was part of that way of life, and was mandated by traditional law and custom.

The common use of the word "subsistence" in English to imply a low standard of living clearly has no application here. In Alaska, subsistence produces an abundance of good food and other products.

There's blueberries, there's cranberries for our bear, and willows . . . and good goose grass in the lake, and there's some just-like-vegetable stuff on the bottom of some lakes that the moose go down and dive for and feed on. In the summertime they really fatten up on it. *(Wilson Sam, Huslia)*

I grew up on the land by the sea . . . living off the fish, the whales, the seals, the eggs, the berries. *(Margaret Oktollik, Kotzebue)*

The peoples do continue to use the halibut, cod, and otters, sea birds . . . kittiwakes, murres . . . and . . . the sea lions . . . the seals . . . the berries. *(Iliodor Philemonof, St. George)*

Fish is our food, bear meat is our food, so is moose. Most of all [we use] the firewood. *(Richard King, Klukwan)*

For Alaska Natives, subsistence lies at the heart of culture, the truths that give meaning to human life of every kind. Subsistence enables the Native peoples to feel at one with their ancestors, at home in the present, confident of the future.

The Economy of Subsistence

The village is a successful, durable, and ancient human invention, and Alaska has some two hundred of them. The majority of the modern world's population lives in villages. These villagers live mainly by direct exploitation of local resources, rather than by selling either their labor or the products of their labor. They also benefit from trade with industrialized society and assistance from central governments (just as cities do) to obtain the range of food, fuel, and services they need today. Dependence on renewable resources continues to define village life. Villages are always changing, but they persist because of their abiding reliance on the land and because of their ability to meet the individual's social, spiritual, and economic needs.

When a White stranger visits a village for a short time, he can no more recognize the subsistence economy on which it is based than a village person, entering a major city for the first time, can understand how its economy can work. The stranger to the village will see only the equipment used for subsistence— snowmobiles, skiffs, nets, sleds, snowshoes, oil drums—and the products of subsistence—racks of drying fish, skins being scraped, smokehouses full of meat. He might guess that the villagers are busy, because he would probably find very few of them at home.

[The Native people] can live off the land. They can survive, just like making an earning, like a White man works; he makes his earning, he feeds his family. The Native people for a long time have survived from the land, just like having a job. That's what they know and they can teach it to their kids. *(Michael Acovak, Sr., New Stuyahok)*

Many White persons imagine that subsistence is merely the act of an individual going hunting or fishing. Subsistence, in actual fact, is a complicated economic system, and it demands the organized labor of practically every man, woman, and child in a village. There are countless tasks, such as the maintenance of equipment (nets, snowshoes, boats, fishwheels, outboard motors, snowmobiles, etc.), preparing the outfit for major hunting and fishing expeditions, setting and checking traplines, dressing and packing hundreds of pounds of meat, cutting and drying thousands of pounds of fish, gathering berries and edible plants, tanning skins and hides, making things from them—clothing, footgear, containers, sleds, tents, kayaks—sharing harvests of meat and fish, and trading with other communities.

Subsistence activities are carried out offshore, both winter and summer, as well as on land, in good weather and in bad. The sea ice off northern Alaska is frozen fast to the land for as long as seven months of the year. Eskimos have always relied on the ocean for most of their food, fuel, and clothing. During much of the year, land-fast sea ice resembles the tundra, and it may be hard to tell where is the boundary between them. Eskimos treat land-fast ice as an extension of the land. They set up camps on the ice; they may hunt and fish and live out there for days or weeks at a time.

Because the products of subsistence activities are not controlled by market conditions and commercial profits nor are they subject to government taxes, it is impossible to say how much these products cost or what they are worth. This feature of the subsistence economy leads bureaucrats to dismiss its importance and makes governments unwilling to strengthen it.

Subsistence is more than a means of production, it is a system for distribution and exchange of subsistence products. The system is not random: it operates according to complex codes of participation, partnership, and obligation. Traditional rules of distribution ensure that subsistence products are available to every village household, even those without hunters.

It has always been our custom to allow the good hunters to catch more than the current limits and share with people who are berry pickers or green pickers or fishermen, who in turn would share their crop and catch with the hunters. *(Darryl Trigg, Nome)*

Sharing is taught early to the young. In this way, the village provides for the elderly, disabled, and needy.

> We share our subsistence foods with one another. Helping one another is natural . . . and is not as difficult as the non-Native help where you have to qualify to receive assistance of one form or another. *(Joe Hotch, Klukwan)*

> If they have too much for themselves for their own family, there is always the sharing. They will either give it to another member of their family, or they will give it to someone else who is really in need. *(Bonnie McCord, Tyonek)*

> For generations passed on, as proud Eskimos, Eskimo Natives as well as Indians and Aleuts, any food caught from the land and water was shared and is shared within the family circle. *(Kenneth Nanalook, Togiak)*

Sustained contact with the outside world has, of course, altered the subsistence economies of every village. Imported goods and food and the introduction of Western social and economic institutions, such as schools, transfer payments, and wage employment, have had many lasting effects. Today, Alaska Natives need a certain amount of money to support their subsistence activities. They must buy equipment, such as snowmobiles, outboard motors, gasoline, rifles, ammunition, and other supplies.

Money enters the village through various kinds of seasonal employment, such as commercial fishing, guiding, firefighting, and construction, work that usually takes the worker away from the village, often for many weeks at a time. Most temporary employment of this kind is based on federal and state capital expenditures. There are very few full-time jobs. Natives employed in the village may include the store clerk, school custodian, and teaching and health aides. Muffy Iya of Savoonga testified that:

> For our local hunters to have successful hunt would require eighteen gallons of leaded gas at $2.55 a gallon for a total of $45.90; three pints of lube oil for a total of $8.25; some shells, which would

cost approximately $50.00, and other necessities for $60.00, which brings a total of $165. And not every hunt is successful.

The investment in money, however, is much less important than the hunter's very large investment of time, labor, hardship, and risk, and it does not alter the fundamental nature of the enterprise. Most villagers do not distinguish conceptually between subsistence and cash elements of the same activity. For example, in the riverine villages, commercial fishing and subsistence fishing with nets occur at the same time and they complement each other: both money and fish are vital to the mixed economy of the village.

It is commonly assumed that subsistence activities are going to be replaced by wage employment. This is not true. The wage-earning population in most villages is a very small percentage of the whole.

Only five to seven percent of the village has jobs here. That means year round. And the rest of the people are the fishermen, which they catch from this bay over here in three and a half to four months. And the rest of the year, there's no jobs. So, therefore, we are relying on subsistence. *(Pete Abraham, Togiak)*

Not too long ago, I made a report for my economics class that put a dollar value on subsistence, and all the meat and all the fish that we eat every year per household would come to about $6,000 to $7,000, and I know we can't afford it. I mean, most of us can't afford it because there's no jobs in the villages for—you know, there's not enough jobs in the villages for everyone. *(Anuska Petla, New Stuyahok)*

Our economic stability in villages is very bad. The unemployment is extremely high. There's no place else in the United States—and maybe in the world—where you're going to find such unemployment statistics as you will in villages. We depend on the food that we get for ourselves. *(Sheila Aga Theriault, Larsen Bay)*

A person unable to set fish traps, hunt, or fish, and without any money, would literally starve. *(Mathias James, Tununak)*

The decline in the revenues derived from Alaska's oil wealth is likely to reduce employment in the villages even further. Subsistence activities offer the only way to employ any substantial number of people in the village.

Subsistence and the Law

Subsistence activities in Alaska are governed by unwritten laws and beliefs that ensure the survival of families and villages. They include codes of customs and behavior that ensure a proper spiritual relationship between humans and animals and conserve resources. They strictly define the rights and duties and the obligations and privileges of tribal members. These laws operate effectively without any system of patents, land titles, or restrictions except self-imposed restrictions that have their origin in the Natives' age-old knowledge of and reliance on the natural world.

> It's unwritten laws that we follow. We don't waste the game, we don't waste the fish, we don't cut down timber for nothing unless we're going to use it, and all that. *(Larry Williams, Venetie)*

Today state and federal laws, which often restrict subsistence activities in the name of protecting them, are in conflict with these traditional laws. Greg Moore, subsistence coordinator for Maniilaq, a Native organization in northwest Alaska, spoke about this in Kotzebue:

> The wildlife regulations interfere with daily life, especially in the villages. Wildlife enforcement efforts target the wrong people for punishment and end up causing more problems than they solve. Wildlife agency personnel are, generally, unprepared and untrained for the human setting of northwest Alaska, so these human problems are not identified and not addressed. Much of what hunters do in the field is technically illegal, even though those same hunting practices are perfectly acceptable from the standpoint of conservation.

Natives from the same region confirmed Moore's testimony:

This subsistence was not very easy to begin with. It has been tough before that [Alaska statehood] because this Fish and Wildlife [Service] has been looking out for us way before that, way before 1971. Sometimes, it gives us three caribou for a season, and look how much that lasts with a big family. It don't last. In the springtime, when we try to go hunt ducks and geese, we have to hide out like the ducks and geese from the Fish and Games, so they don't catch us. *(George O. Cleveland, Kobuk)*

Our lifestyle since 1971 has changed, even our way of life. It is not the same as how it used to be when we were growing up. We weren't told to get so many caribou for our family. Our dads, they would just go out hunting and get however much our families need. But, today, you know, we are limited. They tell us we can get caribou . . . tell us how many to get. So, this has changed. Same way with fishing. Nowadays, they even give you a calendar of how many fish you are catching to keep track. In those days, when we were growing up, that is how it wasn't. *(Genevieve Norris, Shungnak)*

In 1971, Alaska Natives believed that, if they owned their own land, they could protect the traditional economy and a village way of life. Subsistence is at the core of village life, and land is at the core of subsistence. You cannot protect the one unless you protect the other. The law has protected neither.

One of the ironies of ANCSA is that, in Alaska, where the Native peoples live closer to the land and the sea, with greater opportunities for self-sufficiency than Natives of any other state, they have no clearly defined tribal rights, no rights as Native peoples to fish or wildlife. Elsewhere in the United States and Canada, Native communities enjoy special rights. ANCSA extinguished aboriginal hunting and fishing rights throughout Alaska. Native rights now depend on a network of state and federal laws. Caleb Pungowiyi, president of Kawerak, a Native organization, said at Nome:

One of the things that I feel that was a major mistake made by our Native leaders in the Alaska Native Claims Settlement Act was the extinguishment of the aboriginal fishing and hunting rights. I think that this particular section—although they may have been afraid, peoples in the Congress, that it was a management problem, or that there may be some fights concerning the hunting and fishing rights —there probably could have been a mechanism in that the aboriginal hunting and fishing rights could have remained.

Although Native corporations received title to land under ANCSA, they secured no riverine or offshore rights. Fish and marine mammals are not ancillary to land-based resources; in some regions, they make up the greater part of the local diet. In the villages on Kodiak Island, for example, fish and marine mammals account for eighty-four percent of the subsistence diet.

Margaret Roberts of Kodiak said: "I wish that ANCSA could be amended to not only give us our land but also our waters so that we may fish and have our marine mammals that we used to have." Sven Haakenson of Old Harbor agreed: "Give each village a section of the ocean off the three-mile limit." Gordon Pullar, president of Kodiak Area Native Association, urged the establishment of "exclusive maritime zones" for Natives.

The continuing importance of hunting and fishing rights was brought home to me at Togiak, a Yup'ik Eskimo village of about six hundred on Bristol Bay. Before I arrived, the school paper announced a potluck supper "to show Judge Berger the variety of subsistence foods." The whole village turned out for the feast, and two high school seniors escorted me to the head of the line, then to trestle tables laden with food, nearly all of it Native food, with each item labeled: salmon, kelp, walrus, caribou, moose— in all, there were more than twenty Native dishes.

This abundance is threatened. During two days of hearings in Togiak, sixty persons testified, and each of them touched in one way or another on subsistence, and each expressed concern. As Robin Thompson said:

We have many rules and regulations we must follow, and it's getting harder and harder to subsistence hunt. For commercial fishing there should be licenses and seasons, but for subsistence, a way of life, they shouldn't have to buy expensive licenses and wait until seasons to hunt. The Natives know when to hunt and when not to hunt without the seasons posted. Not long ago, the Eskimos would hunt far from Togiak to get moose, deer, and walrus for their families. But now they are being more and more restricted from their natural resources.

These villagers are fighting to protect their right to subsistence. In *People of Togiak v. United States*, they brought a suit to prevent the federal government from delegating jurisdiction to the State of Alaska over the taking of walrus by Natives under the Marine Mammal Protection Act of 1972. The Natives have an exemption from the prohibitions of the act, and they are allowed to hunt walrus and other marine mammals for subsistence, more or less free from external regulation. Notwithstanding this exemption, the state and federal governments had interpreted the act to mean that the federal government can delegate authority to the state to regulate the Natives' taking of walrus. In 1979, the federal district court interpreted a long series of federal treaties and statutes to imply a federal trust responsibility to preserve Native subsistence. The court therefore refused to let the federal government abandon its trust responsibility to preserve Native subsistence values by delegating regulatory authority to the state. As a result, the state relinquished jurisdiction over walrus. In practice, the Natives now regulate the harvest of walrus and other marine mammals by themselves. Congress has since amended the act to facilitate the transfer of this jurisdiction and regulatory authority to the state; the transfer has not yet taken place, and Alaska Natives are vehemently opposed to it.

Togiak may serve to illustrate the history of legislation related to subsistence in Alaska: Natives who depend on subsistence activities struggle to maintain their access to wildlife. Legislators and bureaucrats, meanwhile, in far-off Washington, D.C., and Juneau, transfer jurisdiction over these resources back and forth without regard for the effects on the villages.

Federal laws and policies have recognized the right of Alaska Natives to wildlife for the purposes of subsistence for a long time. As early as 1870, a federal act prohibited the killing of fur seals on the Pribilof Islands by non-Natives, except during certain months of the year, but the act preserved the Natives' right to hunt seals for food and clothing. In 1897, an act recognized the Natives' right to take fur seals by traditional means in the north Pacific Ocean. All of the migratory-bird treaties made exceptions in favor of the Native peoples. Under the International Whaling Convention, 1946, the International Whaling Commission allowed a special exception to enable Alaska Natives and aboriginal peoples in other nations to hunt whales for subsistence.

Although hunting regulations in Alaska have long recognized the Native interest in subsistence, they usually define subsistence in some restrictive way. For example, Native harvesting under the Fur Seal Treaty is limited to traditional means and excludes the use of firearms and power boats. Exceptions in the migratory-bird treaties are limited to a few species. However, the Marine Mammal Protection Act of 1972 recognized the right of Alaska Natives to hunt without restrictions. The act explicitly permits Alaska Natives to take marine mammals for subsistence purposes. Under the act, Alaska Natives are allowed to hunt walrus, polar bear, sea otter, beluga, sea lion, and five species of seal.

ANCSA broke sharply with this tradition by extinguishing aboriginal hunting and fishing rights. Congress assumed that the protection of wildlife resources used for subsistence would be a joint federal and state responsibility. It set the stage for large-scale state and federal intervention in Native subsistence activities. In practice, state and federal policy have provided little protection for Native subsistence activities. Restrictions on such activities were justified on the grounds of biological necessity, convenience of management, and increasing demands by non-Natives for wildlife resources that historically had been committed to Native use for subsistence.

In 1978, the state enacted a subsistence law applicable to all residents of Alaska, Native and non-Native. Under this statute, Native subsistence has not been effectively protected. In 1980, Native and environmental interests combined to ensure that the Alaska National Interest Lands Conservation Act would protect subsistence on federal lands. As a condition of giving the state undivided management of all fish and wildlife within Alaska, ANILCA required the state to enact "laws of general applicability" to guarantee subsistence under state jurisdiction. The state's 1978 law ostensibly fills this requirement.

ANILCA's most important feature is the federal government's recognition of its obligation to protect the subsistence rights of Alaska Natives as a legal imperative deriving from the Constitution. Congress declared that:

> In order to fulfill the policies and purposes of the Alaska Native Claims Settlement Act and as a matter of equity, it is necessary for the Congress to invoke its constitutional authority under the property clause and the commerce clause to protect and provide the opportunity for continued subsistence uses on the public lands by Native and non-Native rural residents.

Congress here found that it is necessary to protect subsistence for Native people on a different basis than for non-Native people. It is hard to see that this was in fulfillment of the purposes of ANCSA, which had specifically extinguished aboriginal rights of hunting and fishing. The significance of the distinction between Native and non-Native users becomes clear in the following passage from the same declaration.

> The Congress finds and declares that—the continuation of the opportunity for subsistence uses by rural residents of Alaska, including both Natives and non-Natives, on the public lands and by Alaska Natives on Native lands is essential to Native physical, economic, traditional, and *cultural existence* and to non-Native physical, economic, traditional, and social existence. [Emphasis added.]

Here is a clear departure from ANCSA. By emphasizing in ANILCA the essential relation of Native cultural existence to subsistence, Congress had returned to the federal tradition of protecting Native rights to subsistence. It is, however, no more than a declaration. Legislation has yet to follow.

The state regime has not worked for Alaska Natives. The issue has been confused by lumping non-Natives and Natives together as "rural residents," an arrangement that undercuts the importance ANILCA gives to Native "cultural existence."

> They came up with a thing called subsistence, or rural residence, and that is not only for Native people but all people who are living

in rural areas. I think that one way to quickly eliminate any of the Native hunting and fishing rights in Alaska is to use the subsistence in the place of aboriginal hunting and fishing rights. *(Bonnie McCord, Tyonek)*

Subsistence, as it is used nowadays, it merely lumps us in. The State of Alaska cannot discriminate, so subsistence is everyone's right. We use the word subsistence in a politically separate term and, in fact, when the state uses subsistence, it is a privilege. To us, subsistence is our inherent right because that is how we have always been and, I believe, that is how we will always be. *(Suzy Erlich, Kotzebue)*

We surrendered our aboriginal rights of hunting and fishing in 1971. Now we depend on state and federal laws. These have brought restrictions. I'm worried that we won't be able to fish in our river here. Soon they'll say, "The Natives don't need fish." *(Lonnie Strong Hotch, Klukwan)*

ANILCA leaves no doubt about the priority, on constitutional, historical, and legal grounds, of the Alaska Natives' right to subsistence. In effect, ANILCA is a partial restoration of Native hunting and fishing rights, but it does not go far enough. More is required if subsistence is to remain a permanent feature of Native life and culture.

Alaska Natives are not prepared to give up their way of life merely because the federal government or the state has passed an unwelcome law or regulation. When a law stands between the Natives and their resources, when it does not take basic economic realities into account, when it conflicts with Native principles or beliefs, compliance with the law is low. Natives do not regard such non-compliance as lawlessness; they regard it as adherence to their own cultural traditions. Athabascans, for example, will take moose for their religious ceremonies, even if they must break a law to do so; Tlingits will use eagle feathers in their ceremonies, even if the federal government forbids it.

Ever since this claims settlement act came, [I've] heard some regulations. Somebody made laws. Eskimos did not make them. We do not go outside of our state and tell other people how they should live. We do not put a limit on how many cattle or how many cows or how much food should outsiders have. We do not make any regulations on that. We do not tell them that they should have this much supply of food. We do not make rules and regulations for them so they will have a limit on . . . certain items of food.

When we try to hunt and provide ourselves and feed our family, our children, somebody comes around and tells us, "If you catch birds, if you catch moose or, if you gather food, we will put you in jail. We have rules and regulations that you have to follow." We do not believe in the rules and regulations, when we try to survive and provide for our family, our own, very own existence. We have been promised punishment for trying to survive. *(Jasper Joseph, Emmonak)*

Regulations that govern Alaska's federal lands set aside for conservation (parks, refuges, monuments, and preserves) are also important to subsistence activities. Federal lands in Alaska, including national parks, are to some extent multiple-use lands. Under ANILCA, the regulations pertaining to lands set aside for conservation are supposed to ensure the continuation of subsistence uses. However, none of these lands has subsistence as its first priority, and subsistence activities on them must always compete with other uses. To protect these competing uses, such as mineral development and tourism, subsistence activities are restricted. Each restriction, singly and in combination with others, erodes the ability of Alaska Natives to survive by subsistence.

National parks represent values that should provide protection for subsistence activities. Much of northwest Alaska, for example, is divided into federal parks, refuges, and monuments. According to Walter Samson, director of lands for the NANA Regional Corporation, the Natives there have access to five federal parks, refuges, and monuments which together comprise millions of acres. "It's a good thing they put up these monuments," he continues, "It keeps people [homesteaders] away from our hunting areas."

But the administrators of parks are concerned to prevent the potential growth of subsistence activities within the parks. They have adopted regulations to freeze subsistence harvests to historical levels and locations, regulations that do not allow for any increase in village populations or possible changes in the distribution or abundance of wildlife resources. Finally, by requiring individual permits for a wide range of activities, including hunting, fishing, cutting wood, and travel, they have changed subsistence from a communal enterprise to an activity permitted and limited to the individual.

Subsistence is a dynamic enterprise, but government regulatory regimes try to confine subsistence activities within a steel web of exact definitions, exact locations, and exact numbers. Such precision cannot respond quickly to ever-changing human needs and environmental conditions.

The Bering Land Bridge Preserve was created, using our village land-withdrawal line as the preserve's boundary. Therefore, our hunting grounds are inside the preserve. The Park Service said they can close the area to hunting and travel, if they feel the resource is being depleted by man and the surface of land damaged by Snogos [snowmobiles] and all-terrain transportations. *(William Barr, Shishmaref)*

We have . . . organizations . . . who worry more about the preservation of a blade of grass or a willow, or some obscure hillside that maybe, just maybe, one out of fifty million people may want to look at in its original state sometime in the future, than about the preservation of our people, our culture, or our heritage. They don't seem to recall that the Eskimo has lived and survived up here for thousands of years without scarring the land as much as they have in just over a hundred years. Before they came with their laws and regulations, there was always a good balance of game to feed our people. It is about time they looked at their own history and worried about the animals that they have eliminated, and leave us to hunt and fish for subsistence. It is a proven fact that the Eskimo has never hunted themselves out of game and probably never will. *(Darryl Trigg, Nome)*

The expansion of government services, ANCSA's division of the land and its resources, restrictions on hunting and fishing, quotas, and competition from commercial fisheries and sport fisheries have reduced some villages to a condition in which their capacity to resist further intrusions and still maintain a Native way of life is seriously impaired. The people of these villages feel aggrieved, for they have had no part in these changes.

> When you take away their pride, and their will to hunt . . . their will to gather their food in their traditional ways, this builds up. This can turn to alcohol, this can turn to drug abuse, and a multitude of other antisocial actions brought onto communities within our region. This, in turn, breeds dropouts in school, which in turn breeds crime, and lackadaisiness. The point that I'm bringing across is that through these constrictive acts . . . without . . . hopes . . . we're still stuck in the mud. *(Guy Martin, Nome)*

> If we can't hunt and fish anymore, if they don't want us to hunt and fish anymore on our land, I hope these people come to us and tell us, show us how else to live. *(Beth Segock, Elim)*

For Alaska Natives, health and well-being are functions of the material and spiritual nourishment that the land provides; ill health and demoralization are results of estrangement and dispossession. Public policy, which we assume to be basically benign, has had consequences in Alaska that are cruel, a policy intended to be passively protective has proved to be destructive in its consequences. As Tom Fields of Kotzebue remarked, "All of a sudden, you take a man, you take the spear out of his hand."

Alaska Natives are acutely aware of the many restraints on their subsistence activities. The loss of freedom to hunt, fish, and trap wherever they wish in the places their parents and grandparents had always used, the limitation of closed seasons, the denial of access to certain areas at any time, and especially the competition from commercial fishermen, sport fishermen, and trophy hunters—these constraints troubled the Native peoples everywhere I went. Laws have protected Native access to some subsistence activities, but laws have not, in general, limited access by other users.

> You can't go out into our bays and walk on a beach without worrying about a bullet go zinging past your head. We have so

many hunters here from the mainland, from down below—and how
come they're coming here to our land? Have we invited them? We
depend upon that land. You go out there now, the deer is scarcer
now and with each year, more scarce. People come down for a
weekend, for two days, come in their planes. They land on our—
on the shoreline. They go walk up and shoot the deer and, with the
snow level coming down, that is the only place for the wildlife to
live, down by the shore, and it's just duck soup for them. They just
go and pick them off. And then where are we left when they go back
home again? The situation may not be irreversible, but it certainly
takes a heck of a long time to heal nature, once it has been scarred.
We have to think about those things because they are playing with
our welfare, the stability of the land that we depend upon. *(Sheila
Aga Theriault, Larsen Bay)*

The sea mammals that we enjoy . . . if the state should take over
the management from the federal government, the fact is, a good
percentage of the populace of the United States of America will
then be coming into the state, into our villages, and deprive us of
our hunting rights. Sport hunters, commercialized hunting, will
then be utilized instead of the Natives, who had consistently hunted
subsistently for their survival. *(Jonah Tokienna, Wales)*

Right now we have more and more sport fishermen coming up here
taking over the streams, and they even fly up to the lakes and, you
know, they carry a lot of fish out of here. And sooner or later, we're
not going to have any left for our people. And they depend on all
this for their living. *(Mary Gallagher, Kodiak)*

ANCSA and ANILCA divided and classified lands that had
hitherto been undivided and unclassified. Boundaries are now
drawn between villages and between regions. Rights to surface
resources are now separated from rights to subsurface resources.
State, federal, and corporate lands are marked off. The surface
of the land supports the many kinds of renewable resources used
for subsistence. The subsurface of the land holds the non-renewable and exportable resources on which the growth of the state
and the Native corporations is predicated. ANCSA aims to replace a viable economic system with another system that, for
villagers, is of limited potential. Land that provides renewable

resources on which the villagers subsist is now considered to be primarily a source of non-renewable mineral wealth.

The Future of Subsistence

Nothing that I have said should be taken as opposition to forms of economic development appropriate to rural Alaska. ANCSA, however, has not provided any significant development, as far as new employment is concerned, at the village level. Villagers will continue to depend on employment provided by government activities; even the private sector in the villages is largely the product of government expenditures. This is typical of remote villages throughout Arctic and sub-Arctic regions, from Alaska to Greenland.

ANCSA simply will not provide new economic opportunities to replace subsistence activities. The villages must, nevertheless, have some economic base, and it can only be a subsistence economy based on fish and wildlife resources. Subsistence is the business of Alaska Natives, and we must give the same diligence that is devoted to the expansion of commercial opportunities to the enhancement of subsistence activities.

It is clear to me that the fish and wildlife resources on which subsistence activities are based must be recognized and acknowledged to be the continuing wealth of the Native peoples. Alaska Natives are already taking the initiative by establishing Native-management regimes.

After the International Whaling Commission's ban in 1977 on subsistence whaling, the Inupiat and the St. Lawrence Island Yup'ik organized the Alaska Eskimo Whaling Commission, which is composed of whaling captains from nine whaling villages. The commission has become an integral part of the international management regime for the bowhead whale; it supervises Native crews and quotas and makes Native knowledge available to national and international researchers.

In 1982, Athabascan Indians and Inupiat in both Alaska and Canada established the International Porcupine Caribou Commission to resist oil and gas exploration and production in the Arctic National Wildlife Range, a development they believe would adversely affect the Porcupine caribou herd on which Natives of both nations depend. This commission is now working toward an international treaty to protect the herd and, in cooperation with the United States and Canadian authorities, it is preparing a caribou-management regime.

In 1983, Eskimos on the west coast of Alaska formed the Eskimo Walrus Commission to represent the villages that take walrus and to develop regulations for this hunt. At present, the commission is engaged in fending off the state's attempt to obtain a transfer of jurisdiction over walrus from the federal government because the state wants to end the exclusive Native right to take these mammals. The commission has also joined with seal hunters to develop a statewide regime for the management of marine mammals.

In 1984, at the initiative of Alaska Natives, the Yup'ik subsistence hunters of several western Alaska villages reached an agreement with the State of California, on behalf of sports hunters within that state, to restrict bird hunting for subsistence in Alaska and bird hunting for sport in California to protect the populations of certain species that had suddenly declined. The agreement avoided the usual federal and state regulatory procedures in favor of a conservation agreement made directly between the users.

Some say that Native people are not good stewards of wildlife resources. I have heard tales of overhunting by Natives. But I have never seen the proof. These tales recur whenever wildlife populations, particularly caribou, suddenly crash. This may be the result of natural ecological cycles. But often such events are attributed to Native overhunting. Usually the true cause does not overtake an allegation made in haste. Ignorance of the migratory habits of these great herds can lead to such accusations. In the late 1970s, Canadian fish and wildlife authorities attributed a sudden decline in the Kaminuriak caribou herd to Native overhunting. Later they found that their census had overlooked tens of thousands of animals.

Self-governing Native peoples have protected and maintained the fish and wildlife resources of Alaska for thousands of years. The unproductive expansion of regulatory processes now threatens, rather than protects, subsistence. Alaska Natives believe they can best protect their interest in subsistence activities through their own governments.

Alaska Natives have always used a variety of customary laws and policies to protect subsistence and wildlife habitat. Ultimately, they seek recognition of their tribal right to wildlife resources and the right to regulate their own subsistence activities.

How should Natives give up their hunting rights? It is well hidden in our mind, and nobody could take it away, like a bird who flies, and nobody could take it or boss it around.

Congress should let the Natives boss themselves, because they have survived during the past. Had to make their own laws then, make their own decisions. That is why they are known to be smart people. That's why they survived in the Arctic for so long. *(Teddy Coopchiak, Jr., Togiak)*

Three /

LAND:

FOCUS OF

CULTURAL CONFLICT

Our land is like our parent. It provides us food, clothing and shelter. Without our land, we would be homeless, we would be like orphans. *(Louie Commack, Ambler)*

ANCSA is the result of an encounter between two very different societies. ANCSA can be understood only in the context of this encounter, this conflict between two cultures. The focus of this conflict is the land.

To one culture, the land is inalienable. Alaska Natives believe that land is held in common by the tribe, a political community that is perpetual. Every member of the community in succeeding generations acquires an interest in the land as a birthright. But to Western society, land is a commodity to be bought and sold. The Native peoples clearly understand that land is at the heart of this prolonged conflict. The protection of their lands has always been their primary concern.

The single biggest fear that we Inupiat have concerning ANCSA is the fear of losing control over our own lands, which we need for subsistence purposes. *(Jimmy Stotts, Barrow)*

I believe that if people, if the vast majority of Alaska Natives, were given the opportunity to either kill or die for their land, that most of them would do just that—if it was that simple. If you were supposed to shoot soldiers, or protect your land with firearms, there are more Natives than the federal government would like to think about that would be more than willing to do just that. The government does not operate in that clear manner anymore. Now, when they are coming in after the land, and they are coming in on these issues, they come not with soldiers but with people carrying brief-cases. If you shoot somebody carrying a briefcase, then you are a criminal, not an act of war. That means that there isn't any clear way for people to protect their land. *(Paul Ongtooguk, Kotzebue)*

If I feel that my people are being threatened from takeover of our lands, I'm going to fight. What I mean is that I'm not afraid for my life, too. The example I'll use is when you go into a grizzly bear's territory. The grizzly bear will be threatened and will fight to defend his territory. I feel that way, too. This is all I have. *(Homer Hunter, Scammon Bay)*

Before the coming of the White man to North America, Native peoples in Alaska, like traditional peoples elsewhere, were orga-nized into political units, self-governing communities that occu-pied a common territory. Native languages have words for these concepts. United States courts have called these political units tribes, and I shall use this word as a convenient way of referring to the institutions the Native peoples—Eskimo, Indian, and Aleut—have established to govern themselves. In Alaska, as far back as 1867, in the Treaty of Cession between the United States and Russia, they were referred to as tribes.

In traditional Native societies, the right to use and occupy land is determined by membership in a tribe. Land is held in common for the benefit of all members of the tribe, and the characteristics of their land define its people.

Our culture comes from that land. That is how we define ourselves as people. That's where we derive our identity. *(Antoinette Halmer, Craig)*

I found widespread evidence that these principles, deeply embedded in Native peoples' culture, are still vital. Native peo-ple do not see land as property to be owned, they see it as the source of life, to be shared by all.

I have to laugh sometimes about ownership of land because, deep down inside, how many of us really think we own it? We want it to be there for use by our people over time, but can we really say that we own something that is God-given? *(Lela Oman, Nome)*

Land is to be shared by everyone. Land is just like the air that we breathe in. Land is like the sunshine that shines on everyone. Land is like the rain that comes down on everyone. *(Andrew Kelly, Emmonak)*

Both village Natives and urban Natives believe the land should be passed on to their children. This spiritual and cultural relationship with the land is the bedrock of Native culture. It has always been so.

Firmly I believe, my personal belief, and the scope of the people that testified here today, that they want to keep the land as a whole, the rivers and the lakes as a whole, to share commonly for generations and generations, as they have done before. *(Kenneth Nanalook, Togiak)*

We thought it was going to be for our children. I remember my grandfather and my uncle saying, it is for our children and grandchildren. *(Celia Marsted, Seattle)*

We have not entered the mainstream, overall, of the society and, culturally, we quite likely, in a lot of aspects, will never want to and don't now. I do feel that we should, whatever comes out of it, we should be able to retain the basic land base for the future generations. *(Sid Casey, Seattle)*

These ideas are not, however, widely understood or appreciated by non-Natives in Alaska or elsewhere in the United States.

Every Native group in the state and every Indian or Eskimo group in the . . . country has a totally different relationship to the land than other people in the Western world. *(Edgar Ningeulook, Shishmaref)*

To the Russians who first came to Alaska, and to the Americans who followed them, land has always been a commodity to be bought and sold. To these very different White nations, land is alienable; indeed, the inalienability of land would impede its profitable use. Alaska Natives reminded me time and again of their quite different views on this subject of central importance to them. As Walter Soboleff said:

> One of our Tlingit laws is that the land for the tribe and clan is inherited . . . land inheritance was endless . . . it was a law of perpetual occupancy.

Taking the Land

Ever since 1492—exactly five centuries ago in 1992—Europeans and their descendants have worked to secure Native lands in the New World for their own exclusive uses. To obtain it, they have tried to persuade Natives to assimilate, tried to inculcate in them European ideas of development and economic progress, the supreme importance of saving, accumulation, investment, and the private possession of land. Columbus, writing in 1492 to the King and Queen of Spain, described the Indians of San Salvador as being, "So tractable, so peaceable . . . that I swear to your Majesties there is not in the world a better nation." Nevertheless, he added they should be "made to work, sow and do all that is necessary and to adopt our ways." Europeans believed they epitomized civilization and preached the only true faith. Without hesitation, they set about the transformation of the New World into their own image.

Again and again, Alaska Natives asked me, by what right did the White people come to Alaska, to seize the land, and to make laws they required others to obey? By what right did Russia sell Alaska to the United States? How could these foreign powers "hand our land over the counter like a toy?"

> People of other nations come to our land and tell us our way of life is the wrong way, what we believed in is not good, what we were doing is not good, because our way of life, our culture, and our tradition on this earth. Instead of going back and trying to improve their own people, they come and tried to improve us. (Axel Johnson, Emmonak)

After the Russians had come and claimed this land without a fight or anything, without asking the people if they could sell it or not, they just went ahead and sold this land that belonged to our forefathers, Eskimo people, to what they called the United States. They sold for money. They sold this land, which is ours and belonged to our forefathers since time immemorial. The Russians . . . sold our land to the U.S. government for money, even if it was not their land. *(Rudolph Williams, Emmonak)*

By what right did Europeans and their American descendants dispossess the Indians? In 1823 Chief Justice John Marshall enunciated the rule of discovery in *Johnson v. M'Intosh.* According to this view, Europeans had discovered America, an achievement that gave them sovereignty over the indigenous people, dominion over their lands, and the exclusive right to acquire title to these lands. But, Marshall added:

[The Indians] were admitted to be the rightful occupants of the soil, with a legal as well as just claim to retain possession of it, and to use it according to their own discretion; but their rights to complete sovereignty, as independent nations, were necessarily diminished and their power to dispose of the soil at their own will, to whomsoever they pleased, was denied by the original fundamental principle that discovery gave exclusive title to those who made it.

The right of discovery, according to Marshall, conferred on the government of the United States the power to convey title to the land, but Marshall also acknowledged that, under United States law, the Indians retained an exclusive right to use and occupy the same land. Only the government could acquire this aboriginal title from the Indians and, until the government had extinguished aboriginal title, no one other than the Natives themselves could legitimately use or occupy Native lands. Marshall's rule of discovery still serves as the basis for aboriginal claims in United States law. Leaving moral obligations and high-minded concepts of abstract justice to one side for the moment, the common law of the United States acknowledges that the original inhabitants have a legal claim to their aboriginal lands. This aboriginal title had first to be extinguished before others could legitimately use these lands, and only the government could extinguish aboriginal title.

But historical events and conflicting philosophies have often obscured the law. Whether Englishmen exploring westward, or Russians pushing toward the east, Europeans have long believed that they had a duty to develop the earth's resources, a duty that justified them in their successive dispossessions of the Native peoples. Some European philosophers considered American Natives to be subhuman. Such a people, "having no government at all," said Thomas Hobbes, could therefore have no rights.

Another principle at work here is the European idea of increase or growth. Land should be worked for the profit it could yield; an owner who did not profit from the land did not deserve to hold it, justification—if one were needed—for taking the land from Natives who were plainly unable to profit from its use in the European sense.

> It could be for no other reason than money that the White men have started fighting . . . for our dear old land here. The White men try to collect money and put the money in the bank, and whatever is put in the bank belongs only to them. But the Natives of Alaska used the land only for survival. . . . The bank was for everyone, not just one person. *(Jens Flynn, Tununak)*

Spain had struggled to impose some kind of order on White-Native relations, to ensure that Native rights were not wholly ignored. Its efforts were, in the main, unsuccessful, and Spanish settlers in the New World contributed a chapter to Spanish history that has come down to us as the Black Legend. North of the Rio Grande, Native tribes, hunters, gatherers, and agriculturalists, were dispersed about the continent. The first French and English arrivals were primarily interested in furs, and they established formal trading relations with various tribes. The objectives of the fur trade were best met by keeping the Indians on their land. When settlers arrived, however, they considered the continent to be a wilderness waiting to be tamed. Pioneers, moving across the continent, made clearings in the forest and broke sod on the plains. Towns sprang up, some of which became centers of distribution in the nation's network of domestic trade. Changes of this sort exemplify European ideas of progress.

How does a society that claims to be based on the rule of law justify the taking of Native lands for homesteading, building railroads, or producing oil and gas? Some theorists have relied on God's commandments and on Christianity's civilizing mission. Others have referred to the greater obligation to dedicate the land and its resources to agriculture and industry rather than to hunting and gathering. John Winthrop, the Puritan leader, combined both arguments: he argued that the Indians had only a natural right to as much land as they had improved or could improve and that the rest of the country lay open to any who could and would improve it. "If God were not pleased with our inheriting these parts," he asked, "why did he drive out the Natives before us?"

The European nations interested in the New World espoused the rule of law; all were Christian, all regarded themselves as civilized. Each of them issued declarations, some of them promulgated laws to uphold the moral obligation to deal fairly with the Indians and not to take their lands without consent. In 1542, Spain passed the New Laws to ensure that Native land rights would be respected. But the Spanish in Mexico and Peru paid no attention to them. The settlers in Mexico threatened to revolt against Spanish authority; in Peru they did revolt. The New Laws went unobserved.

It was impossible for the authorities in Spain to enforce fair dealing in the New World. Neither could the United States, two hundred years later, enforce fair dealing in its own back yard. Congress, in the Northwest Ordinance of 1787, insisted that in dealing with Indians, "in their property rights and liberty the Indians never shall be invaded or disturbed." The settlers simply ignored the ordinance, and Congress could not or would not enforce it.

President Washington was troubled by his government's inability to protect Indian tribes. He despaired of "anything short of a Chinese Wall, or a line of troops" to keep land speculators and squatters out of Indian territory. Henry Knox, Washington's Secretary of War, was responsible for Indian affairs. He wrote:

The desires of too many frontier white people, to seize, by force or fraud, upon the neighboring Indian lands, has been, and still continues to be, an unceasing cause of jealousy and hatred on the part of the Indians. . . . As we are more powerful, and more enlightened than they are, there is a responsibility of national character, that we should treat them with kindness, and even liberality. It is a melancholy reflection, that our modes of population have been more destructive to the Indian natives than the conduct of the conquerors of Mexico and Peru. The evidence of this is the utter extirpation of nearly all the Indians in most populous parts of the Union. A future historian may mark the causes of this destruction of the human race in sable colors.

In the end, of course, White settlers secured nearly all of the Indian territory they wanted. Their motives in taking it were various, and many persons, officials and ordinary citizens, tried to mitigate the harm that White occupation of the continent was bringing to the Indians. Their attempts usually entailed serious and sustained efforts to make the Natives over in the image of the White man. Every such effort reflected the dominant culture's idea of the life to which Indians should aspire. The Indian way of life was entirely based on subsistence activities, which required unfettered access to large areas of land. Subsistence is impossible where land has been divided into privately held units suitable for agriculture.

The federal government acceded time after time to the removal of Indian tribes as agricultural settlement pushed the Indians off their fertile lands. Although Andrew Jackson's name is indelibly associated with the policy of removal, it had been Jefferson's policy, too. Jefferson was deeply concerned by the questions of legality and morality presented by the seizure of Indian lands, and he devoted much of his second Inaugural Address to relations with the Indians who lived in territory covered by the Louisiana Purchase in 1803.

The aboriginal inhabitants of these countries I have regarded with the commiseration their history inspires. Endowed with the faculties and the rights of men, breathing an ardent love of liberty and independence, and occupying a country which left them no desire but to be undisturbed, the stream of overflowing population from other regions directed itself on these shores; without power to divert, or habits to contend against, they have been overwhelmed by the current, or driven before it; now reduced within limits too narrow for the hunter's state, humanity enjoins us to teach them agriculture and the domestic arts; to encourage them to that industry which alone can enable them to maintain their place in existence, and to prepare them in time for that state of society, which to bodily comforts adds the improvement of the mind and morals. We have therefore liberally furnished them with the implements of husbandry and household use; we have placed among them instructors in the arts of first necessity; and they are covered with the aegis of the law against aggressors from among ourselves.

While urging the Indians to accept and adapt themselves to the White man's civilization "to maintain their place in existence," Jefferson instructed the War Department to remove the Indians beyond the Mississippi. He justified this policy, which might in a president less revered seem hypocritical, on the grounds that the alternative would be extermination of the Indians by land-hungry frontiersmen.

Events were to bear Jefferson out. Few settlers were prepared to countenance the assimilation of Indians if that meant Indians could keep their land. The Cherokees, for example, became farmers; they had schools and other White institutions. Assimilation was not enough. When settlers wanted their land, the Cherokees were removed from it.

Even beyond the Mississippi, the Indians were not safe. The California gold rush in 1849 and the general belief in the Manifest Destiny of the United States brought new encroachments on Indian land there. A new policy of establishing reservations turned out to be a different form of removal. Once the Indians were placed on reservations, lands outside the reservations were opened to settlement.

After the Civil War, Indian reservations, ranges, and hunting grounds were scattered over the western United States. The Homestead Act of 1862 encouraged widespread settlement in the West and, in 1869, the first transcontinental railroad was completed. To allow the Indians to continue to hold fertile lands encompassed by their reservations was contrary to the idea that land should be made available for ranching and agriculture in the name of progress. Indian use of the land gradually gave way to the inexorable demands of White settlers. In 1871, a congressional committee reported:

> No proposition is better established in the American mind than that the welfare of a state and happiness of its citizens require that the lands be held in private proprietorship, and in tracts sufficiently small that each may be cultivated and managed in person by its individual owners.

Beneath this rationale lay an irresistible drive to seize Indian land. The taking of the Black Hills from the Sioux illustrates the point. Despite a federal treaty with the Sioux Indians, White prospectors had rushed into the Black Hills on the Sioux reservation to search for gold. In 1877, President Grant, in his last State of the Union address, referred to breaches of the treaty. The Indians, Grant said, were not safe from the "avarice of the White man" who had "violated our treaty stipulations in his search of gold." Having condemned those who had invaded Sioux territory in violation of the treaty, Grant said, "The question might be asked why the Government has not enforced obedience to the terms of the treaty." Troops had evicted the first prospectors to enter the Black Hills, but then "gold had been found in paying quantity, and the effort to remove the miners would only result in the desertion of the bulk of the troops that might be sent there to remove them." Grant concluded these remarks with the observation that "all difficulty in this matter has, however, been removed—subject to the approval of Congress—by a treaty ceding the Black Hills." Aboriginal title, solemn treaties, and the goodwill of presidents were never enough to protect the Indians.

In the mid-1880s, the Indians on their reservations were still holding land that Whites wanted for settlement. In 1887, Congress passed the General Allotment Act, also called the Dawes Act, after its sponsor, Senator Henry L. Dawes of Massachusetts. Its supporters claimed that individual proprietorship of land was necessary for the Indians to advance toward full participation in American life. The act authorized the division of communally held reservations into individual parcels or allotments of 160 acres for each Indian family head and eighty acres to each single Indian over eighteen. Congress wanted the Indians to give up hunting and fishing to become farmers. Once the reservations had been divided among members of the tribe, the remaining land could be declared surplus and sold to White settlers. Some reservations were not divided into allotments, and the land remaining from those that were divided was not always declared surplus and made available to settlers; in some cases, it remained in tribal ownership. Nevertheless, the act's impact on Indian life and Indian land was enormous.

The United States held the allotment in trust for the Indian for twenty-five years, during which time it could not be alienated, encumbered, or taxed. After twenty-five years, the Indian received a fee-simple patent to the land. The General Allotment Act received support not only from settlers eager to obtain surplus Indian land but also from Whites who were anxious to find some way to ensure that the Indians might be allowed to keep at least some of their land.

President Theodore Roosevelt acclaimed the General Allotment Act to be "a mighty pulverizing engine to break up the tribal mass." But tribal life proved to be far more durable than Congress anticipated. The legislation did not achieve its main purpose, the assimilation of the Indians, because it did not take into account the basis of Indian cultural life—tribal identity. In any event, much of the allotted land was unsuitable for farming, Indians had little experience of farming, and Congress never appropriated sufficient funds to enable them to buy adequate farming equipment. Federal restrictions on the transfer of allotted land made it difficult for owners of allotments to dispose of land during their own lifetime. When the original holder had died, his allotment was divided among numerous heirs. After one or two generations, there might be hundreds of heirs, a fact that caused serious problems of management and gave little or no return to individual owners of ever-smaller parcels of land.

According to the Meriam report, "The Problem of Indian Administration," published in 1928, the act, far from improving the lot of Indians, had left them worse off than ever. Former tribal lands were now occupied by White settlers. Land patented to individual Indians had, often without their knowledge, been sold for non-payment of taxes. Indians had been persuaded to sign documents conveying title to land without realizing what they meant. Between 1887 and 1934, total Indian landholdings had been reduced by ninety million acres, more than twice the land conveyed by ANCSA to Alaska Natives in 1971. Even these statistics are misleading because the lands the Indians lost were the most valuable lands they had owned.

In 1934, Congress attempted to redress the effects of the General Allotment Act by enacting the Indian Reorganization Act (IRA) to halt further allotment of Indian reservations and to revitalize tribal governments. In testimony before the House Committee on Indian Affairs, John Collier, Commissioner of Indian Affairs, deplored the great loss of Indian lands under the allotment act and voiced the urgent need to reverse this trend.

Through sales by the Government of the fictitiously designated "surplus" lands; through sales by allottees after the trust period had ended or had been terminated by administrative act; and through sales by the Government of heirship land, virtually mandatory under the allotment act; Through these three methods, the total of Indian landholdings has been cut from 138,000,000 acres in 1887 to 48,000,000 acres in 1934.

These gross statistics, however, are misleading, for, of the remaining 48,000,000 acres, more than 20,000,000 acres are contained within areas which for special reasons have been exempted from the allotment law; whereas the land loss is chargeable exclusively against the allotment system.

Representative Edgar Howard, co-sponsor of the Indian Reorganization Act and chairman of the House Committee on Indian Affairs, addressed the House on the day the act was passed:

So far from being a means of civilizing the Indians, [the allotment act] soon became a perfect tool for the capture of Indian lands. As soon as the Indians had begun to receive their unrestricted patents, they flocked in great numbers to the real-estate agents and the land seekers and parted with their deeds for small sums of ready cash.

Or if the original allottee had died before his trust period expired, and he had numerous heirs, lineal and collateral, as was usually the case, it became necessary to sell the land in order to partition the estate. As if this method of capturing Indian lands were not working fast enough, the Government adopted the further policy of disposing of the so-called "surplus" lands of the allotted reservations.

As a result of this system, the allotted Indian reservations are in general riddled by alienations, the extent of the alienation being almost exactly proportionate to the length of time since the original allotment was made. The Indians of many tribes have lost practically every square foot of land they owned. Many reservations have in Indian ownership a mere fragment of the original land.

Even if Indian allottees retain their land after receiving fee patents, the heirship system inevitably leads to the ultimate loss of land. Even the first generation of heirs is usually so numerous that physical partition of the land is impossible and it must be put on the auction block to divide the estate. What little land actually descends to heirs of the first generation will almost inevitably be lost through partition among the second generation. We are thus headed for the complete wiping out of the entire Indian estate unless the system is changed.

ANCSA has many parallels to the General Allotment Act. It places the land in fee title, it makes land alienable and taxable. Although ANCSA has not divided the ancestral lands of Alaska Natives into individual parcels, it has made Native land a corporate asset and divided its ownership into individual stock certificates. These shares are not tangible like land but, after 1991, they can be sold. Even if shares are not sold, corporations could lose their lands through bankruptcy, corporate takeovers, and tax sales. Christine Smith, a law student from Fairbanks who is studying in Seattle, said:

I disagree very much with the concept of corporations for American Native groups, just like the time of the allotment era, when land was given away to individual Indians in the Lower 48 in an attempt to make them into farmers. I feel like the corporate structure is given to us, to make us businessmen and businesswomen. I don't know about you, but for me and for my family, it doesn't work very well.

We do not learn easily or remember well. During the 1950s another attempt was made to break up the tribes and tribal landholdings. This was the termination policy. It began in 1949 with the Hoover Report on the reorganization of the executive branch of the federal government. Among other things, the report recommended that Indians be integrated into the general population as full, tax-paying citizens. A number of congressional enactments terminated federal programs for specific tribes, transferred lands out of tribal ownership, and extended state jurisdiction over Indian lands. The policy did not last long, but it did a great deal of damage and produced fundamental changes in the patterns of Indian land ownership. It was against this background in the late 1960s that deliberations began that led to ANCSA.

The best-known victims of the termination policy were the members of the Menominee tribe. Under the Menominee Termination Act of 1954, the tribe's landholdings of 234,000 acres in Wisconsin were transferred to Menominee Enterprises, Inc., a state-chartered corporation. Members of the tribe received restricted stock certificates in the corporation, but effective corporate control was in the hands of a voting trust managed by a Wisconsin bank. The certificates that represented shares never became transferable because Wisconsin passed laws every two years to make them non-transferable, but the possibility always existed that this stock, representing control of all the tribal land, might go on the open market.

According to a congressional report in 1973, the termination plan "brought the Menominee people to the brink of economic, social and cultural disaster." Under corporate control, a thriving sawmill operation became only marginally successful. Menominee Enterprises, Inc. was burdened with corporate debt, a difficult management scheme, and high county and state taxes. It went to the verge of bankruptcy, and 9,500 acres of tribal land owned by the corporation had to be sold to pay interest on bonds and tax obligations. This transaction was bitterly opposed by the great majority of tribal members.

Under the termination policy, a number of tribes besides the Menominees were terminated. Some of them, including the Menominees, have since had their tribal status and tribal lands restored. But for others it is too late now, their lands have been alienated and tribal members dispersed.

The structure of the Menominee Termination Act is strikingly similar to ANCSA. Willie Kasayulie, president of the Akiachak tribal council said "[ANCSA] is a Menominee Termination Act in disguise to terminate Alaska Natives." In both cases, state-chartered corporations rather than tribes hold the land; shares are issued; afterborn children are excluded as shareholders; the stock eventually becomes transferable; and the land becomes taxable. In 1973, Congress intervened to provide for the restoration of the Menominees' tribal government, thereby averting a certain loss of land.

The Conflict in Alaska

Imagine a map of Alaska, with Native settlements marked along the coasts and rivers, and patterns of traditional use, occupation, and trade represented to show Alaska as it was before the Russians came. In those days, geography and climate were effective barriers to White advance. Successive waves of economic exploitation began with Russian traders and colonists in the late eighteenth century. They moved in a great arc along the Aleutian Islands to Kodiak, along the coast of south-central Alaska, until they reached southeast Alaska. They hunted the sea otter nearly to extinction, and they nearly exterminated, by the introductions of European diseases, the Aleut population, which dropped from about fifteen thousand to less than two thousand, but they did not take the land away from the Natives.

During the nineteenth century, commercial whalers and fishermen began to visit Alaska's coasts. Then, in the late 1800s, gold was discovered. The miners spread from southeast Alaska through the interior until they reached Nome. The turn of the century saw the first large-scale federal land withdrawals to create parks, refuges, and national forests; the withdrawals included a large petroleum reserve in remote northern Alaska. The military occupation of Alaska during the 1940s led to land withdrawals throughout Alaska for military bases and installations. By the mid-1950s, the timber industry was entrenched in southeast Alaska and, in 1959, the state began to make land selections under the Statehood Act. In 1968 came the discovery of oil deposits on the North Slope.

In 1966, also, Secretary of the Interior Stewart Udall imposed a freeze on land transfers to protect the Eskimos and the Indians in the possession of their own lands. Here was an Alaska version of the "Chinese Wall" to which President Washington had wistfully referred. In 1971, when Congress passed ANCSA, some thought of it as a barrier to further encroachment on Native lands, but ANCSA is a barrier designed to fall of its own weight.

ANCSA extinguished aboriginal title and conveyed fee title to Natives organized into private, profit-making corporations. The spoken and unspoken assumption was that the Natives would use these corporate lands for mineral exploration and production and other forms of economic development. The state continues to select its lands using criteria based largely on natural resource potential.

Another concept has also been gaining ground—conservation, the idea that land should be preserved in its natural state. The United States invented the national park in 1872 with the creation of Yellowstone National Park. Just as many persons regard Alaska as the last great storehouse of mineral wealth, many others regard Alaska as the last great storehouse of wilderness land in the United States. Under ANILCA, the comprehensive federal conservation statute passed in 1980, new federal parks, refuges, and monuments have been created and old ones have been extended. Protected land of this kind now includes more than 100 million acres in Alaska. The designation of wilderness lands may also impinge on the Native way of life, because some environmentalists deplore—and try to limit— Native use of parks and refuges for subsistence activities.

Alaska has had its own allotment act, though its effect has been limited to date. Passed by Congress in 1906, it allowed Native families to claim 160 acres of land. Few Alaska Natives applied; but in the late 1960s, they were advised that allotments would be unavailable after Congress had enacted a settlement of land claims. Faced with this deadline, thousands of Natives applied. Today there are approximately ten thousand allotment applications pending. Many Natives told me they are pursuing their applications because, if ANCSA lands are lost, they will still have some land to pass on to their children. But the allotments, if they are approved, especially those at strategic locations, are likely to be put up for sale and to pass from Native control. They will play their part in the process of breaking up communally held land.

The map of Alaska is now filled up, each townsite color-coded. Has this brought security of tenure to the Natives? Not according to Tommy Ongtooguk of Kotzebue:

> We did not have a concept of boundaries, of unseen lines traced over the earth and dividing the land. . . . If someone established a fish camp, it was considered that person's or that family's fish camp. It was permanent in everyone's mind and considered settled. Now with deeds, lawyers, and the BLM [Bureau of Land Management] who can be sure of anything?

Federal policy in Alaska has always perceived the Native peoples to be poor, backward, and uncivilized, anachronisms in a modern world. Their backwardness is demonstrated by their inefficient use of land. Such cultures, such peoples, making idle use of valuable land, must give way to the far more profitable uses to which the White man will put the land.

The treatment of aboriginal title by the courts illustrates this point. The Supreme Court of the United States has consistently said that the Indians' right of occupancy is "as sacred as the fee simple of the Whites." But in 1955, in *Tee-Hit Ton v. United States,* a case arising in Alaska, the Supreme Court held that Fifth Amendment protection against taking land without compensation did not apply to Indian lands held under aboriginal title. The title was recognized in law, but it could be extinguished without compensation. No land but Native land in the United States would have been denied Fifth Amendment protection.

Attitudes are more important than constitutions, laws, and

regulations. Analysis of the legal reasoning of the court's decision does not explain why it reached this conclusion, but the fact
is the Supreme Court was unwilling to enforce the Fifth Amendment for Indians. If the judges in the *Tee-Hit Ton* case had
perceived Native society and values as authentic, they would
have had no difficulty extending Fifth Amendment protection to
Indian land in Alaska held under aboriginal title. Farmers living
on the land are entitled to protection under the Fifth Amendment, but Indians living off the land are not. The legal arguments are pure sophistry. The fact is, judges believe that one
form of land use and occupation—ownership, if you will—is
valid, whereas the other is not; one way of life is valid, the other
is not.

Here, I suggest, is the reason why Congress decided on a
corporate model of landholding for the Native peoples living in
two hundred remote villages in far-off Alaska. Congress was not
altogether ignorant of conditions and life in rural Alaska, but
it did not wish to acknowledge the legitimacy of Native ways of
life. Alaska Natives were a problem to be solved, and Congress
thought it knew how to solve it. The solution has made land the
focus of cultural conflict in Alaska.

We have, since the passage of the land claims act, we had forced
upon us a new definition of land use and ownership. The people
in this area, as well in other villages in the state, who live off the
land used all aspects of the land. They camped in certain areas and,
when they camped there, the people respected that particular camp
site. Maybe next year you wouldn't be there, so somebody else
would be there. This new definition with Native allotments and
federal lands, state lands, corporate lands, has brought many problems to our areas. *(Ron Schaeffer, Kotzebue)*

When you look through the corporate eye, our relationship to the
land is altered. We draw our identity as a people from our relationship to the land and to the sea and to the resources. This is a
spiritual relationship, a sacred relationship. It is in danger because,
from a corporate standpoint, if we are to pursue profit and growth
—and this is why profit organizations exist—we would have to
assume a position of control over the land and the resources and

exploit these resources to achieve economic gain. This is in conflict with our traditional relationship to the land. We were stewards, we were caretakers and, where we had respect for the resources, that sustained us. *(Mary Miller, Nome)*

The state surveyed and divided lands without regard to natural features, such as the course of rivers and their associated drainages, that are important to subsistence activities. For Alaska Natives, it was an inappropriate model of land survey and selection. Under ANCSA, Native corporations were allowed to select lands to be surveyed in townships. The selection process required difficult decisions. Should a village corporation select land traditionally used for hunting and fishing or land to be used for economic development? The two types of land are not often the same. Different uses will affect land in different ways, and once made, the choice is usually irrevocable. Some regional corporations had to choose their lands on a checkerboard basis because their selections conflicted with state-selected lands. This practice prevented the acquisition of large blocks of holdings and it kept access open to state lands.

The land it allocated to Native corporations is inadequate to sustain Native subsistence activities. Weaver Ivanoff, president of Unalakleet's tribal government, said: "Many valleys and rivers are lost to us. You can see our markers still. We fished there, we hunted there—but it's not ours anymore." Others echoed this theme:

I believe the amount of land that we received is only a small portion of what we actually used for subsistence purposes. Fifty percent of our village withdrawal was in water. I think this was an oversight on whoever came up with the land claims act, and I, as a board member at that time, wanted to select nothing but water as protest, but we had to go by the sections within the act from the front page working towards the back. But we definitely don't have our prime subsistence grounds within our village land selections. I would like to go on record where our primary place for subsistence activities will show and be proven that they are outside the village withdrawal areas, and there are limitations and restrictions put on by whoever owns the land, either be it state or federal government. It can get to a point where we can no longer hunt, fish, or gather, if these different land managing agencies feel that we are depleting the game resource or damaging the land that they manage. I definitely feel that we did not get enough ground to protect our interests for self-preservation. *(Henry Ahgupuk, Shishmaref)*

Although, as property owners, Natives have the exclusive right to wildlife on their own land, they have no rights as Natives for hunting, trapping, or fishing reserved for them over the ninety percent of Alaska in which their rights were extinguished. Even on Native lands, the state asserts its jurisdiction over fish and wildlife.

ANCSA was the first settlement of aboriginal claims to choose the corporate model and to make the land a corporate asset.

I think that ANCSA will never fully to the extent advocate and stand individually for the real Native part of us. I think that ANCSA is not totally Native. It is written in the Western-adopted ways, and it has that business nature where the land is collateral, just like a car or anything. Anyone, in one way or another, gambles with it, and Western laws apply to it. We have a limited say on it. The ANCSA—if it has to be there—it should be for the good, to help us but not take away our way of life.

This is the Native personal part of us. Talking about land is about our everyday, individual part of us. Our ancestors survived because of the land. A large portion of our diet today still comes from the land. What if, sometime in the future, the food is still on the land, but our land is taken away and in the hands of others who wouldn't permit us to go out and hunt for the game, etc. With no money to pay to hunt, if that was the only way. I think, in this modern day and age, you have to pay for everything. What would we do? *(Virginia Commack, Ambler)*

The corporate model required by ANCSA will not only affect future uses of Native land, it will also disrupt the scheme of ANILCA, whereby the federal government has tried to preserve more than a hundred million acres of land in its natural state. Here, at least, federal purposes are compatible with the Native ethic of conservation. The preservation of land in its natural state can be consistent with Native hunting and fishing for subsistence. In fact, many lands set aside by ANILCA are contiguous to lands held by Native corporations. If Native land passes from Native ownership and is opened to the development of minerals and other resources, it will place federal parks, refuges, and monuments at risk, too. Native lands in the hands of developers will constitute bridgeheads to contiguous federal lands, and those who are trying to turn federal parks over to private development will be that much closer to their goal. This should be a matter of concern to all Americans.

Many parts of coastal Alaska, including open water and land-fast sea ice, are natural extensions of the land base used by Natives. The Natives apply the same rules of communal ownership and utilization to marine resources as they do to terrestrial species. The transformation of a natural resource, whether it be land or wildlife, into a commodity that can be alienated threatens the communal life of the people who use it and increases the likelihood that Native access to fish and wildlife resources will be lost.

The alienation of resources used in common has led in Alaska to the division of access to the commercial fisheries. In 1974, the state adopted a limited-entry scheme to regulate commercial fishing rights. Fishermen received individual transferable rights to fish based on their past participation and dependence on the fishery. Many Native fishermen, who did not fill out the requisite forms, did not receive their permits.

What has happened to the permits the Natives did receive? Figures issued in September 1984 by the Alaska Commercial Fisheries Entry Commission are unsettling. Between 1975 and 1983, Alaska Native permit ownership declined by 752 permits or 13.8 percent. The most lucrative fisheries (Bristol Bay, Gulf of Alaska, and southeast Alaska) witnessed an even greater decline, 18.5 percent. The biggest decline occurred in the most lucrative fishery of all, the Bristol Bay salmon fishery, where Native-owned permits dropped by 21.3 percent.

The situation in some villages is even more disturbing. Robert Willard of Angoon testified that he opposed limited-entry permits when the idea was under consideration in 1974.

I was one of three people that testified against the limited-entry system. I think, sadly, that my testimony bore out that. In my little village we had thirty-three vessels. . . . Presumably they would have been eligible for limited-entry permits. And there were seventeen that qualified under the system. Today there are only two.

Many witnesses in other villages, bitter about limited-entry permits, were quick to draw parallels to ANCSA.

A few of the families that needed the cash sold them [limited-entry permits]. With limited entry, big money started coming in. So what difference will there be with the stock in 1991? *(Schwal Enukwuk, Manokotak)*

It's going to be like fishing permits. Fishing permits, initially, were controlled by the Native people, but fishing permits got sold as people are under the pressure of a cash economy. They've sold their fishing permits, and I think it's going to happen with shares of regional stock. *(Joli Morgan, Bethel)*

It will not do to dismiss the sale of these permits, like the sale of shares, as a matter of personal choice. Both situations represent the division of what the Native peoples regard as a common resource into distinct units of individual wealth. For whatever reasons—deeply rooted cultural attitudes, the fact that they need the money—these permits are drifting from Natives to non-Natives.

ANCSA has made Native land a corporate asset and, like limited entry, it has allocated individual rights or shares to Native people. These shares become, after 1991, alienable units of wealth. I think that shares in the Native corporations will pass from Native into non-Native hands. With them will go control of the corporations and the land. Lands used for subsistence activities will be lost, thereby disrupting forever any possibility of self-sufficiency and eliminating at a stroke the cultural heritage of Alaska Natives. A matter of personal choice? The choice will be made for all future generations of Native peoples of Alaska. Many Natives told me that they believe no one should have the right to make that choice.

The attitude of most Whites, whether trying to preserve Native culture or to eradicate it, has been in general a patronizing one, dismissing the idea that Native cultures are still viable today. Persons who regard extension of the commercial and industrial system to Alaska as the very definition of progress regard Native societies as poor and acutely disadvantaged, anachronisms in a modern world. Persons who regard the traditional past of the Native peoples as a time of happiness and social cohesion often wish to see them protected from White society in a kind of living folk museum.

These two ideas, Progress and the Noble Savage, are both creations of the Western imagination. Proponents of both ideas conveniently assume that Native cultures are static and unchanging, that the Native peoples themselves are locked into the past. Such an assumption can become self-fulfilling: if Native peoples are not allowed the means to deal with present-day problems on their own terms, their cultures may in fact tend to become degraded and static. Time and again, during my journey through the villages, the people in them insisted that their culture is of the utmost importance in their lives. The failure of White people to acknowledge this fact constantly forces the Native peoples to defend the legitimacy of their cultures. Pete Schaeffer said in Kotzebue:

Historically, land has been taken from Native tribes for about 250 years, and with the White men's belief in their myth of Manifest Destiny, it is possible that they will continue to do so for as long as it takes for them to own everything. As long as they can profit from whatever is on or below the earth, they will not stop. Unfortunately, God chose to put a wealth of natural materials in our land and, like a magnet, the wealth attracts those who have no honor or respect for the people who live on the land. Systematically, they conspire on the easiest way to get the land. What they dreamed up was a plot for that purpose and, amongst it, was the Alaska Native Claims Settlement Act.

His powerful conclusion cannot be ignored.

The total disregard for people with cultures of their own and, in fact, their tendency to despise different cultures is ignorance of the worst kind when, in fact, indigenous cultures are developments in body and spirit that were best for the use of the land and constructed for countless ages.

Four /

1991:

THE UNRAVELLING

OF ANCSA

"It's like cancer. We got something we didn't want. We're just sitting around 'til doomsday in 1991. *(Kenny Sam, Huslia)*

Under ANCSA's terms, on December 18, 1991, the Native corporations are required to call in all their shares. On January 1, 1992, they are required to issue new shares that will not be subject to any restrictions as they are at present. After 1991, shareholders will be free to sell all or any portion of their shares, to pledge them as collateral, or to use or dispose of them in any other way. The Native corporations can then become targets for takeover. Furthermore, the land, twenty years after its convey-ance, whether developed or undeveloped, becomes taxable. If the state or local authority levies taxes and they cannot be paid, land can be taken. In every village I visited, Alaska Natives expressed fear that their ancestral lands will be lost after 1991.

Non-Native Alaskans, bemused as they have been by the Native corporations and their financial saga, are beginning only now to comprehend that, to Native Alaskans, the success or failure of the corporations is not the paramount issue, except as it bears on the question of land. Even now, more than one regional corporation and many village corporations are in dan-ger of going bankrupt. After 1991, the risk of bankruptcy will multiply.

After 1991, there will also be the possibility of takeovers of Native corporations and Native land. This has made Alaska Natives fearful.

We are concerned about 1991, how we, the villages, the Native villages, are going to be affected by that. *(Michael Hunt, Kotlik)*

The biggest issue that I see before me now is 1991, and I don't believe it is a stock issue. For me, it is the land issue because the people who do hold stock hold title to the land, and when that stock is sold, traded, or revested back to the corporation, so does their right to that land. *(Dean George, Angoon)*

But there is another view held in Alaska. Many non-Native Alaskans believe that in 1971, ANCSA settled forever the claims of Alaska Natives. The Natives received money and land, and legislation has extinguished any further claims they might have had. Now, the popular thinking goes, we can get on with the business of developing Alaska, unimpeded by Native claims and unobstructed by Native enclaves. Such persons believe that the best use the Natives could make of the money they received in compensation and the lands to which they received title is to invest them both in economic development, an object that is plainly, as they see it, in the best interests of all Alaskans, including Alaska Natives. There may be risks, but risk is in the nature of American enterprise. No one, they imagine, is obliged to sell shares and, if the Native peoples decide to sell them and thus dispose of their land, it is their own free choice. As for taxes, all other Americans pay taxes, and why shouldn't the Natives? So runs the popular view.

The Native peoples of Alaska, however, want to hold their ancestral land in trust for future generations. If shares can be freely transferred, then control of shares that represent the land can be transferred out of Native hands. At every village meeting I held, Alaska Natives overwhelmingly rejected the idea that shares could unrestrictedly be transferred.

Alfred Wells, at Noorvik: "If we sell to millionaires from outside, there'll be No Trespassing, No Trapping, No Hunting signs." Rena Ballot of Selawik: "All Natives should get together and put [their stock] where they can't sell it. There should be no selling to Whites." Harry Nashiknik at Barrow: "Nothing can come out of selling shares." David Greist, Selawik: "We want something written into the act where you can't sell your shares."

After 1991, when we are able to sell our shares . . . and perhaps have our land taxed, what little we have left, we may never have anymore. . . . What little we have left could only be protected by restricting, absolute restriction, of selling our shares to outside of our Native people. That is one of the only few solutions. *(Alice Tucker, Emmonak)*

One hundred shares represents the past life of the Native people, it represents the culture, the land, lifestyle, village living. And this portion, this hundred shares, is something that's going to become available for sale to the public in 1991. One of the things that one of our shareholders said at one of the annual meetings was that . . . he didn't think he had the responsibility to hold a hundred shares in his hand that represents the Native people throughout the ages in his village and area, to give him the opportunity to sell that in 1991. He said that is something that never should have happened. And he said that, as a young man himself, that he does not want to have that responsibility, has not earned the responsibility to even speak at an annual meeting or at a table that has decisions made at. And I think that he is speaking true. I don't like the responsibility of holding a hundred shares that I could sell and other shareholders could sell in 1991. Because what is sold there is the end of the people. . . . The people would continue on living, but what is taken from them is everything that they lived for, land and everything that comes with the land. *(Sam Demientieff, Fairbanks)*

I feel like, you know, if they sell their stocks they would be selling their culture. They would be selling their land, their heritage. They would be left with nothing, and I don't think that should even be considered because, after we lose our culture and our heritage, what else do we have? *(Myra Starkloff, Tyonek)*

I certainly don't feel that any individual Native . . . the temptation will be great in 1991 to sell stock. And I don't feel that anyone, no individual Native, has the right to sell that stock, because no one has the right to sell the future of the kids. *(Paul Blank, Seward)*

I feel that our children is not going to have that opportunity to receive our stocks when it is sold to somebody else. We are going to be hurting the rights of those children. *(Clifford Weyiounna, Shishmaref)*

Congress conferred shares on all eligible Native persons living on the date ANCSA was enacted. They would be the only
shareholders to receive shares without having to pay for them.
This inevitably excluded children born after that date. With a
profit-making stock corporation, there could be no continuous
process of enrolling infants to receive stock without having to
pay for it. Such an action would reduce the value of the present
stockholders' shares and eliminate the point of having a stock
corporation in the first place.

Risks to Native Land

In the Lower 48, generally the federal government holds the
land of Native Americans in trust for the benefit of the tribes
on the reservations. In Alaska, state-chartered Native corporations now hold Native land as private land in fee simple.

This exposes Native ownership of land to certain dangers.
There is the possibility of corporate failure. A bad debt that a
corporation incurred in a real-estate venture in Anchorage, for
example, could result in the loss of land used for subsistence by
Natives in some distant village who are unaware of the risks
their corporate activities may involve. At present, the land of
Native corporations can be seized and sold to service unpaid
debts or to satisfy creditors in case of bankruptcy. Charlie Edwardsen, Jr., of Barrow suggested that "the gains under ANCSA
are going to be lost in bankruptcy court." Bankruptcy would
continue to be a risk after 1991, even if the prohibition on the
sale of shares were continued. So long as a corporate model is
the vehicle for holding Native lands, they will always be at risk.

Native corporations have always had the right to sell their
lands and some have already sold parcels of land in the ordinary
course of business and at a profitable return. These sales are
exceptional. Some have begun to sell land to meet current ex-
penses. More are going to have to do the same. Indeed, the
obligation to recall shares in 1991 and to issue new shares in
1992 is likely to require professional assistance that some village corporations will not be able to afford. They will be spending their last few dollars to place their assets in jeopardy.

Then there is the possibility, after 1991, of corporate take-overs through buying up of the shares held by Alaska Natives. Not only the shares at present held by individual shareholders will go on the market after 1991. The corporations will be free to issue new stock, a common way in the corporate world of raising capital. In that event, large blocks of shares might be taken up by banks, underwriters, and other investors. Any buyer who acquires enough (it need not be a majority) of a corporation's shares to control it would, in effect, control its assets, including land.

According to ANCSA, corporate lands will become liable to state or local taxation twenty years after their conveyance. As originally enacted, ANCSA prohibited taxation of undeveloped ANCSA lands until 1991, but because of delays in conveying the lands selected, Congress amended ANCSA in 1980 to extend the tax exemption for undeveloped lands to twenty years after the date on which the corporation received title to it. So, much of the undeveloped land will become taxable during the 1990s.

In a state that is extraordinarily dependent on revenues from a single source, oil from Prudhoe Bay, and whose revenues are already in decline, the possibility of a tax on Native corporate lands seems very real. If a state or local property tax were imposed on lands used only for subsistence or, for that matter, on any lands, developed or undeveloped, that were not generating income, they could be lost through tax sales.

> The village corporations will not be able to meet or pay that tax sooner or later, and the land from the villages will be lost bit by bit, by not being able to pay the taxes. *(Henry Ahgupuk, Shishmaref)*

> Once they start taxing the corporation land . . . I mean, how we gonna pay for it? We just have to tell state, "Well, there's a certain amount of land here that we have to give to you ordinary, to save our corporation land." And if it's taxed every year, before it's over with, it seems to me that state will have all the land back anyway, and that we won't have. *(Carl Charles, Dot Lake)*

> I wonder if the government realized that, by taxing the land, eventually they'd get it all back? Because, how are most corporations going to pay taxes on that land? It's such a large amount of

land. I just don't see how they expected people to be able to pay taxes on it. . . . I really do believe that most of the land will revert back to the federal government, or the state government, because of corporations' inability to pay taxes in the future. It might not happen in 1991, but it will happen. *(Vicky Hykes, Unalakleet)*

As far as 1991 goes, and them paying taxes, or charging taxes, and we have to pay taxes on it, there's got to be some sort of way, through politics and bureaucracy, which I'm sure you know a lot more about than me, that we can get around that. We got to find that way. So that way . . . we can pass that land on to our children and their children so we could keep up the heritage and culture. But we can't pay taxes on it. That'll just force us to sell the land to pay the taxes. And then eventually we'll have no land again, and then there goes our culture. *(Mike Vigil, Chenega)*

ANCSA has exposed the Natives' land to other risks, but here are the principal ones: corporate failure, takeover, and taxation.

Some Conventional Solutions

Some persons think that no changes need be made in ANCSA and that the existing corporate structure can be made to work. Louis Thompson, president of the village corporation of Kassan, says that ANILCA gives the Native corporations the tools they need to deal with 1991. He refers to certain amendments that Congress passed in 1980 to enable corporations, before December 18, 1991, to limit voting rights to Native shareholders. Non-Native shareholders could acquire stock in 1992, but they would not be allowed to vote it. These amendments also allow a corporation to require that any stock put up for sale must first be offered to the corporation or to the shareholders' immediate family. In this way, the corporations would have the right of first refusal and the right to match a price the shares could obtain on the open market. At Saxman, Reynold Denny says:

And, after 1991, if they start selling their shares, what I like to see, the [Native] corporation buy back the shares that the people have; instead of having it sold outside to White people. But I'd like to see the Native corporation to keep this within the Native people, their corporation. To keep it going. If they sell it to anybody outside, pretty soon the corporation will be overrun by White people. There's lots of White people that would like to get in, as I can see, try to get in any way they can. That's why I'd like to see the Native people buy back the shares that belong to the corporation members. That's what I'd like to see happen. Otherwise if they start selling their shares outside to some other people, pretty soon there won't be no Native corporation here.

But Native corporations would not ordinarily have the cash to buy out shareholders who wish to sell. Andrew Hope III of Sitka says the right of first refusal under ANILCA "is an empty promise . . . because I think everybody realizes by this time that a right of first refusal is virtually worthless to . . . a Native corporation that doesn't have the ready cash of an outside invader." By way of illustration, Roger Snippen, president of the Sitka Native corporation, says that the Weyerhaeuser Company or any other large corporation could outbid any Native corporation, including Sealaska. His point is well taken. Horace Biederman of Eagle considers that:

> It would be right to have the right of first refusal, but I don't believe that it's going to be physically possible for some corporations to meet this need, because I believe that we don't have the money to do this.

Andrew Gronholdt, a board member of the Aleut Corporation, says: "I think, if a corporation will have to buy back—I don't think they're going to have enough money."

Charlie Johnson, president of Bering Straits Native Corporation and chairman of the Alaska Federation of Natives, Inc., insists there is among shareholders an expectation of individual benefit that must be dealt with. Larry Peterson of Fairbanks said that he was opposed to any limitation on the right to sell shares. "If they can't sell their stocks, then what is the land claims for?"

Some regional corporations have advanced the idea of selling shares back to the corporations before 1991. This suggestion is quite different from a right of first refusal. It would permit the corporation to make an offer to buy out shareholders who want to sell their shares. No one else could make an offer for the shares. Under this scheme, shareholders could obtain cash for their shares, but they would still have the right to buy them back at a later date. But persons without regular income who sell their shares are unlikely ever to be able to buy them back. There is a real possibility that many shareholders will sell their shares for very little because there is no true market for them and no possibility, until after 1991, of an offer based on market value. If a great many shareholders in a corporation sold out, the few Natives who had retained their shares—and they might be very few—could, in the end, gain effective control of the corporation and its land.

If shareholders sell their stock, they will create another class of Natives whose descendants will swell the ranks of Natives without any legal rights in the land. The distinction between two classes of Natives might be exacerbated by inequalities of wealth: the poor, who had to sell their shares to the rich, who would own and control the corporations. This sort of outcome might be in keeping with American ideology, but it would not be in keeping with the ideology of Native communities.

ANILCA authorizes private landowners (in this case we are talking about the Native corporations) to enter into agreements with the federal government or with the State of Alaska (if it decides to participate) to place private lands in the Alaska Land Bank. Native corporations that deposit their lands in the land bank are granted immunity from adverse possession, real property taxes, and court judgments. The idea is to protect lands used for subsistence.

Lands subject to this agreement must be managed by their owners in a manner that is compatible with a management plan used on adjoining or affected state or federal lands. Agreements can be made for ten years with the possibility for renewal every five years. There are, however, some restrictions: lands may not be developed, improved, mortgaged, or sold either prior to or while subject to the agreement. Although the owner must provide access to federal agencies to enable them to administer their own lands, to conserve fish and wildlife, and to carry out other obligations, the agreement cannot require rights of public access as a condition for accepting land into the bank.

So far, no Native corporate or other private lands have been placed in the land bank. A proposed agreement between the National Park Service and Gana-A' Yoo Ltd. (a merged corporation of the Galena, Nulato, Koyukuk, and Kaltag village corporations) stalled in July 1984 because of the terms specified by the Department of the Interior. Of greatest concern was a requirement by the department to give access to the general public, even though this requirement flies in the face of the statutory provisions. Most important of all, federal agencies, whose policies may well restrict subsistence activities, will manage lands in the bank.

But the land bank, even though it requires that subsistence land be preserved, does not protect the corporation that owns the land against the possibilities of bankruptcy and outside takeover. A trustee in bankruptcy might not be obliged to renew the deposit of land in the land bank, and an outsider who took over the corporation would be under no such obligation. Moreover, simply by paying any back taxes, new management of the corporation could remove subsistence land from the land bank at will.

The Dilemma of Stock Sale

1991: It seems a long way off, and yet it is so close! Why was 1991 set to be the deciding factor on how I should handle my stock in the Atxam Corporation and The Aleut Corporation? It is absolutely unfair to me that I should decide what I should do with my stock I own in these corporations, when I don't even understand what it is all about! I'm only starting to understand, and I'm sure the average American, who deals with stocks can make a good decision on what he wants to do with his stock. But as for me, well, I can only say that I'm beginning to basically understand what it means! (George Kudrin, Atka)

When I visited Klawock in southeast Alaska, a quiet hearing suddenly became charged when two witnesses said they would willingly sell their shares after 1991. Both of them said they had received no benefits as stockholders in the corporations. Elwood

Thomas, a veteran of the land-claims struggle, asserted that he would "seriously consider selling my shares while there's still some value to these shares." John Scan said he "would not hesitate to sell because the stock has done nothing for me to date."

Their statements provoked an intense response. Pauline Peratrovich, a grandmother, said that she wouldn't sell her shares; her people had fought for the land, and she thought it should be passed on to her children and grandchildren. Jim Martinez, a fifty-year-old logger, spoke with great force. He said the land had belonged to the Tlingit for many years. The fight over the land is not over, and he believes it will go on for years. Fran Sanderson said, "We do not want the land to go. Ever. Because we believe that our land should go to our children and their children after them." Mary Brown, president of the village chapter of the Alaska Native Sisterhood, followed:

> I had all kinds of things that I wanted to say, but I just can't get it all together right now. But my feeling is, I'm not selling my stock and neither are my children—if I have anything to say about it—because this is our land. And whether or not the government ends up taking it away from me, I want to feel good inside myself that I kept my land until I couldn't hold on to it any more, and not because I had to sell it, but because it was taken from me again, like it was taken from me before. And what I have now, I'm going to fight to keep.

Some witnesses considered that, if the corporations become successful and pay dividends, the shareholders will have confidence in them and will not sell, but not everyone agreed.

> I think if the fact that a person sees that his corporation is very successful, and he realizes that his hundred shares in 1991 is worth a lot more money than an unsuccessful corporation shareholder, he's going to probably sell out too, if he sees fit. (Sam Demientieff, Fairbanks)

Whether a corporation is successful or not, whether it is paying dividends or not, many shareholders will be tempted to sell their stock. In either case, there will be reasons to let the stock go.

How can we expect Alaska Natives to behave like shareholders in some ways, and not like shareholders in others? The Native peoples' most important concerns have nothing to do with shareholders' attitudes or with the corporations' prospects. Right now, they focus on the tension between cultural values and immediate economic needs.

Sometimes people believe in a general principle and yet . . . when they're in a tough spot, they might do something because they just don't have any choice. *(Eunice Nesseth, Kodiak)*

It seems to me that when the time comes, it will depend on the intensity of the loyalty. . . . Some will say, "I will sell." Another will say . . . "My inheritance is not for sale." *(Donna George, Gulkana)*

I don't think the majority of Native people are going to be wanting just to get rid of their stock. But on the other hand, there is a lot of people that, you know, if this thing doesn't have any results, they're going to—they have needs. They have needs that have to be taken care of. *(Pat Isaacson, Manley Hot Springs)*

At Haines, David Light said, "I circulate around a lot of my friends, young guys like myself, and a lot of my friends are going to sell their shares. That's what they say. It scares me." I asked him why. "They want the money. They want to buy a car. They want to get nice-looking clothes, I guess. They want—some of them want to travel. And some of them already have buyers lined up."

Excluded Natives

In settling the aboriginal claims of all Alaska Natives, ANCSA conferred direct benefits of the settlement only on Natives who were alive on December 18, 1971. Only they shared in the distribution of cash. Only they received shares. But the Native tribal systems all recognize that future generations have as great a right in the land as the present generation. Dividing

Natives with whom the settlement was made in 1971 from Natives born after that date has created two classes within the same community. In Huslia, Dorothy Attla said there are 492 shareholders, but already there are 140 children who are not enrolled, a number she believes could double in another thirteen years. In Emmonak, Jim Carden, a White teacher and eight-year resident of the village, told us that, of 207 students enrolled between kindergarten and grade twelve, 98 are shareholders and 109 are non-Natives under ANCSA's terms. Included among the non-Natives are his own two children, "born of a Yup'ik mother," but born too late. A Native child who was born on or before December 18, 1971, is a shareholder; a student sitting at the next desk, born the following day, is not. Virtually all Alaska Natives who testified in the villages found this situation deeply disturbing.

It's pretty hard to take when you have a son that's two weeks too late, and he asks you, How come I'm not a Native? That's—you know, that's hard. *(Helen Weiss, Port Lions)*

I would like to see an amendment in the ANCSA act providing an inclusion of the others, including the children born after 1971 or as they are called, "afterborns." It is not fair for them to be excluded from their own heritage. . . . The Natives of Alaska have always shared, sharing is our way. It will never change. ANCSA has reversed our heritage by not providing for our own children. *(Chuck Newberg, Shishmaref)*

When shareholders die, they may leave their shares to their children. In this way, future generations will acquire shares. But receiving shares by inheritance is bound, over time, to create inequalities among shareholders and to undermine the cohesiveness of the village: a couple with ten children may divide their shares equally among them, whereas a couple with only one child may leave all their shares to that child. The children of the second generation, in these two examples, will have twenty shares each in the first case but two hundred in the other. In succeeding generations, the disparities will be even greater. Moreover, increasingly smaller divisions of

the shares will reduce dividends, already trivial, to insignifi-
cance.

> I am twenty-two. How would I divide my shares if I was to have,
> say, ten children [her mother has ten children], and later they
> give their children their shares that was given from me. There
> wouldn't be much left. Or the after-borns, who by some chance
> do not receive shares—what will they do? *(Lily Walunga, Gam-
> bell)*

Under the General Allotment Act of 1887, land descended to
the allottees' heirs in ever smaller interests. After a few generations, the existence of hundreds of heirs caused overwhelming
problems of management and little or no return to the individual
owners. Because ownership of the land was fragmented into ever
smaller units, the land was no longer available for communal
purposes.

The same thing happened among the Osage Indians, who had
a reservation in present-day Oklahoma. In 1904 and 1905,
substantial discoveries of oil and gas were made, and the Osage
tribe accumulated a large trust fund in the United States Treasury from the sale of oil and gas leases and other assets. In
1906, Congress passed a statute to individualize Osage tribal
property and to authorize a roll of the tribe's members who were
entitled to share in distributions of cash from the fund. Income
from the fund was paid out on a per capita basis to the persons
on the membership roll or to their heirs.

The distinctive feature of the Osage scheme is the use of a
tribal roll established in 1906 to serve as the permanent basis
for per capita distributions of tribal income and property. Osage
Indians born after the roll was closed did not acquire the usual
rights of a person born into an Indian tribe to share in distributions of tribal property. Only those who were on the roll in 1906
were entitled to receive distributions. This right, now called the
Osage headright, passes to their heirs. The right to vote in Osage
tribal elections depends on headright ownership. Today, most
persons of Osage descent own no headrights, receive no tribal
income, and cannot vote in tribal elections. Some persons own
more than one headright, and some own fractional shares of

headrights; some headrights are owned by non-Osages. The parallels with ANCSA are plain.

As time goes on, it will become increasingly difficult to expect the Natives who received shares under ANCSA to reduce the value of the assets they control by sharing their ownership with children born after 1971. This problem could have been avoided, had the settlement been based on traditional forms of tribal membership. After all, membership in a tribe depends on who you are not what you own. Membership in a tribe cannot be bought and sold like membership in a corporation, which is a form of property. Witnesses in every village made clear to me their conviction that children born after 1971 should be allowed to participate fully in the Native corporations by virtue of who they are.

Those who are born after '71 should have a share in this. *(Iliodor Philemonof, St. George)*

We all think that all Natives should have equal shares, even the afterborns. *(Geraldine Kelly, Emmonak)*

Just because you were born later, that doesn't mean you . . . you're not Native. And I think that's what the land claims is all about, you know, for all Natives—not the ones that are just born before 1971. That's the way I feel about that. *(Evelyn Higby, Point Hope)*

Even though, if we give the younger people stocks, even though it will decrease the money that we get from our stocks . . . we didn't really have to do anything to get these stocks. We should share it with people who are Natives, too. *(Bobby Stephan, Tyonek)*

We need to find some way to enroll our children that were born after the closing dates—so important. They're part of us—they need to be able to identify with something and somebody. And I think being members of our Natives' organizations and being a part of the land, they can identify. *(Eleanor McMullen, Port Graham)*

Only seven more years be 1991. They said . . . if we let them in, that's going to water down everybody's share. Hey, water it down! *(David Light, Haines)*

Many Alaska Natives favored the automatic addition of new shareholders born after 1971. But the idea is impractical and defeats the purposes of a stock corporation. If Congress were prepared to authorize a shareholders' corporation with an open roll, to allow the issue of shares by right to newly born Natives, no stockholder could know from day to day the extent or the value of his shares. If, on the other hand, the rolls were opened, then closed again, there would still be a class of excluded Natives born after the new date.

Arguments over the rights of non-shareholders to use Native-owned lands for subsistence will arise, and the corporation must decide who will have these rights. The rising generation, or members of it, could be excluded. Natives holding the largest number of shares may assert a claim that will be difficult to deny to a larger share of scarce resources. The problem of children born after 1971 and the inevitable creation of inequalities through inheritance are the causes of division and dismay among the present shareholders of the village corporations.

Here we are labeling our afterborns non-shareholders. Already I have heard of rivalries in families because of this. I have fears that eventually it will separate us as families. Parents, grandparents will have to take the blame, although we are not at fault—all because of those few select people who made the decision for us. *(Arlene Ongtowasruk, Shishmaref)*

I have four children right now, and not one of those four children are eligible to participate in my corporation. I perceive that as totally causing dissension in the village and causing untrust. I see it as in the future, the village . . . would hardly work together, in the future, because of those things. *(Bonnie McCord, Tyonek)*

Doing Nothing

What will happen after 1991 if no solutions are found? Is the Native fear that shares will be sold and their lands lost unreasonable? To answer these questions, we should look at earlier per capita distribution schemes, beginning with the General Allotment Act of 1887.

That act led to the loss by Natives of ninety million acres of land. The resemblances between that act and ANCSA are so great that, if the lessons of history have any meaning, they indicate that, in the years after 1991, Alaska Natives will sustain heavy losses of Native land.

Should anyone think that much has changed since the General Allotment Act was passed ninety-eight years ago, consider the recent example in Alaska itself of the limited-entry fishing permit and the value it has conferred on fishing permits. Their value has led permit holders to sell them to non-Natives, and I think we will see the same thing happen to ANCSA shares. The connection between a limited-entry permit and earning a living from fishing is clear, but the number of them that Natives have sold is alarming.

I think a very good parallel is what has happened with the limited-entry program in Alaska. The studies show that the permits that were granted to Alaska Native people, they are being transferred away into people from outside the state in great numbers, so that it's going to be—the larger number of the people that own the rights to fish in the state are going to be—from the cities or even outside the state. . . . People fall into hard times, and they see a source of ready cash. And those things can be picked up for a lot less than they're actually worth. And I think that this is one of the problems that the stockholders—if the provisions for the sale of stock isn't changed, the same thing's going to happen here, so that eventually the people that do retain their stock are not going to necessarily have control of the corporations that they belong to. But it'll be somebody else that has stepped in and gotten the majority control. *(Roy Madsen, Kodiak)*

We have seen, for instance, the fishing permits, both on Kuskokwim River and the Yukon River, that have been put on the market. If that is any indication of what's going to be happening, if the shares are put on the market, then we will indeed have some people who are really in a hardship. Now that we are getting into a cash economy more and more every day, there will be a tendency of the people to put their shares on the market. That is my personal feeling. *(John Paul Jones, Bethel)*

Because there is no direct link between shares in the corporation and earning a living, the shares are likely to be sold sooner and in greater numbers than were the limited-entry permits.

The experience of the Canadian Métis is also a compelling example. In 1870, after an uprising, the government of Canada agreed to give the Métis, a population of mixed Indian and White blood that considered itself to be a distinct aboriginal people, 1,400,000 acres of public land in present-day Manitoba. The federal government delayed providing title, and it substituted scrip, a certificate that entitled the holder to so many acres of land or to a sum of money. Scrip was negotiable, as ANCSA shares will be after 1991. As White settlers poured in from Ontario, most of the Métis, who were buffalo hunters, sold their scrip (usually for very little) and moved farther west to the valley of the Saskatchewan, ahead of the wave of settlement, to continue to hunt buffalo. By 1885, settlement had caught up with them. The Northwest Rebellion ensued; it was put down and the Métis leader, Louis Riel, was hanged. Afterwards, more scrip was issued to the Métis; in fact, the federal government was dispensing scrip across the plains until 1908. Often the Métis sold their scrip in order to get through the winter.

John A. Macdonald, Canada's first Prime Minister, insisted that, having accepted scrip, the Métis had ceased to have any rights as aboriginal people. For more than a century, the federal government refused to negotiate with the Métis. Their population has increased, and the Métis continue to insist they are a distinct people and entitled to their own land, even though many of their ancestors, perhaps most of them, took scrip at one time or another and then sold it. In April 1985, a century after the Northwest Rebellion, Prime Minister Brian Mulroney and the provincial premiers met with Métis leaders, and the Prime Minister agreed that the Métis are entitled to a land base. Allotments, limited-entry permits, scrip, or shares—attempts to divide property held in common—do not alter the way that Native people regard themselves or their land.

Alternative Institutions

Now that Alaska Natives understand more clearly the implications of ANCSA's corporate structure, no one should be surprised that they feel the deck has been stacked against them. In the words of Jim Martinez of Klawock:

Just like the government's saying here, we'll let you have this land for twenty years. You can play around with it, and do whatever you want with it. But after twenty years, we're going to get it back.

Some critics of ANCSA have suggested that the only solution to its problems is to restructure the settlement by transferring the land held by corporations to other institutions. State Senator Frank Ferguson, a board member of NANA Regional Corporation since its establishment and president of the Alaska Federation of Natives, Inc. from 1980 to 1983, says:

The land and natural resources so close to the Native people will eventually get tied up by outside interests through the economic infrastructure of the corporate world.

For the Native people to retain their legitimate legal status to their land under the Native land claims settlement act, the majority of lands selected must be clear of political and economic pressure and a land patent given to the Native people of Alaska in perpetuity. Anything else will eventually lead to assimilation of these lands into something the Native people were fighting to prevent with the request for a land settlement.

The alternative institutions most often suggested are non-profit corporations, cooperatives, and tribal governments. Non-profit corporations and cooperatives fall under state law, but tribal governments come under federal law. How much protection does each of them offer against the dangers of corporate failure, corporate takeover, and taxation? All three of the suggested institutions qualify as membership organizations. The principal distinction between them and a profit-making corporation is that membership in them is not transferable, whereas members of a profit-making corporation hold shares that can be bought and sold.

Under state law, non-profit corporations cannot issue stock or distribute assets as dividends. They can, however, derive income from their assets and provide benefits to their members or to a larger group, benefits that usually take the form of public services. If their lands are used for religious, educational, or charitable purposes, they are exempt from local property taxes. Local governments have the option of granting further exemptions if corporate lands are used for community purposes.

On the other hand, non-profit corporations are not subject to many procedural regulations that are designed to protect individual shareholders from a profit-making corporation's improvident actions. For example, Alaska corporate law protects dissenters' rights and requires a minimum quorum of thirty percent for voting on the alienation of all or substantially all of a profit-making corporation's assets. For non-profit corporations, the minimum quorum is only ten percent, and there are no dissenters' rights; theoretically, as few as five percent of the members can dispose of all the corporation's assets. On the positive side, membership organizations that give every member one vote cannot be taken over by outside interests, although, like profit-making corporations, they can go bankrupt and lose their assets to creditors.

A cooperative is a not-for-profit corporation that can undertake profit-making activities. As long as it does business with only its own members, then in theory its activities will not generate income or profit for either individual members or the corporation because, in doing business with only its own members, the cooperative generates savings, not income. These savings may be distributed to the members of the cooperative either in cash or in kind. Because these distributions are the product of savings, they can be excluded from the income declared for federal-tax purposes, and they are not taxable in the hands of the cooperative. A cooperative may also do business with non-members but money earned from activity of this kind is profit, and it can be taxed as income.

Cooperatives are usually formed to fulfill one of three general purposes: to market a product, such as crafts or agricultural products; to provide members with supplies needed for a particular enterprise such as wholesale groceries or cattle feed; or to supply members with a particular type of product such as retail groceries or particular kinds of equipment.

Although a cooperative may sell stock to raise revenue, the stock generally cannot be voted, and control of the cooperative

remains with its members. Cooperatives, being membership organizations, are not susceptible to outside takeovers, but they
don't afford the range of protection to shareholders that is characteristic of profit-making corporations. Like non-profit corporations, they can be structured so that as few as five percent of the
members can dispose of the assets. Cooperatives do not afford
any special protection against bankruptcy or against forced or
even voluntary liquidation of assets, nor are there any general
exemptions from property taxes.

Non-profit corporations and cooperatives, although they
afford protection against takeovers, do not afford protection
against the threat that bankruptcy poses to the Natives' land nor
protection from the threat of taxation. Although non-profit corporations may be exempted from property taxes in certain cir-
cumstances, there is no assurance under state law that lands
used for subsistence activities will always be exempted from
taxes. Cooperatives have certain income tax advantages, but no
general exemption from property taxes.

Tribal government, not surprisingly, is the alternative most
often brought up at the hearings I held in the villages. It is the
only one of the three possibilities that offers the advantages of
a membership organization and would also protect Native land.
Tribal governments have sovereign immunity from lawsuits.
Under the federal Indian Reorganization Act of 1934, applied
to Alaska in 1936, tribal governments organized under the act
are also guaranteed the power to "prevent the sale, disposition,
lease or encumbrance of tribal lands, interests in lands, or other
tribal assets without the consent of the tribe."

Like non-profit corporations, tribal governments can provide
services to their members, and they can receive tax-deductible
donations to finance the services that a government usually
provides. They are authorized under the Tribal Governmental
Tax Status Act to raise revenue to provide such services by the
sale of bonds. Tribal governments can engage in profit-making
activities and they can distribute any surplus to their members;
as governments, they are exempt from federal income tax on
their profits.

Tribal government would afford protection against the loss of
Native lands through corporate bankruptcy, takeovers, and taxa-

tion. Because membership in the tribe is perpetually renewed, the land would pass from generation to generation. Tribal government would bring Alaska Natives into the mainstream of federal Indian law. It might also entail, although it need not, federal trust ownership of Native lands.

Measured against the wishes of Alaska Natives past and present, ANCSA is obviously flawed. I do not wish to suggest that, if worst comes to worst, the land will be lost on the morning of January 1, 1992. But a process of retreat will begin as Native-owned land passes from the Native sector to the non-Native. No institutional arrangements have been made to check this inevitable process, which is implicit in ANCSA.

For Alaska Natives, the loss of their lands would be catastrophic. The severance of ties with traditional life and the foreclosure of any possibility that the villages might achieve a greater measure of self-sufficiency would have serious implications for non-Native Alaskans, as well. Without its Native villages, without the subsistence way of life, Alaska would not be Alaska. This would be a great loss not only to tourists and other visitors, but to the very idea of Alaska itself. Without Native villages, this wild and rugged country would become an antiseptic wilderness. Alaska is very much an urbanized state. It is the Native people that constitute the permanent rural population of the cold, isolated regions. This physical separation is a fact of life in Alaska. If they lose their land, Alaska Natives who now live in villages would drift to the cities in ever larger numbers and become a financial burden on the state. Moreover, the presence in urban surroundings of an embittered Native population would make impossible the achievement of a partnership between Natives and non-Natives that is still possible in Alaska.

THE HEARINGS

Young and old attended the public hearings, and I welcomed them all. Bill Hess traveled with me, first for *Tundra Times*, later as an independent journalist and photographer, to hearings held in many parts of Alaska. Here are some of the excellent photographs he took during these travels. About half of them were taken during a boat journey I made in 1984 to hear testimony at villages and fish camps along the Yukon River. The accompanying testimony comes from hearings throughout the state.

Hamel and Sonja Frank, Venetie   *Sam Newman, Juneau*

I think that we are really fortunate to be given the time to speak up and address how we feel, how we personally feel, even though for a lot of us and I can say that for myself, it is really hard to come up and try to address your personal feelings. (*Marie Schwind, Kotzebue*)

> Might say, that this is a good vehicle, a good time for us to say our feelings to the rest of the people in the region; where we are now and what we can do about it. (*Tom Fields, Kotzebue*)

I don't look at Mr. Berger as a person that is going to miraculously turn things around. He can only rephrase what, ultimately, all of us as individuals and collectively decide is going to happen next in how we view our world. That world can be as small and narrow as we interpret it, or as wide as the world view that we have or the universal view that we have. (*Dennis Tippleman, Kotzebue*)

This is a good start, anyway. It's a good, truthful start, just to find out what everybody thinks and do something that's going to be productive for all of us; not only us but the ones after us and everything, to keep it intact. (*Lester Erhart, Yukon River*)

I'm glad at least I talk a little bit that you hear me, you hear me saying what I think. Thank you very much. (*Richard King, Klukwan*)

She said that she usually doesn't speak in public but she said as she looked around at people's faces she said that she's looking at her friends. (*Martha Neck, Togiak*) [Translated by Rev. Andrew]

I think this thing with having people come from the other Native villages is just fantastic because here we are in Larsen Bay, and we think our problems must be the only ones like them any place, but I know in every other village we're all dealing with the same thing, and if we get our heads together periodically and talk about it among ourselves and decide what to do and then back that decision up all the way, I don't think it's too late. (*Sheila Aga Theriault, Larsen Bay*)

Emmonak hearing

Glenn Fredericks at Sleetmute

Myra Roberts, Venetie
Copyright © 1985 by The Tundra Times

Winnie Billy, Emmonak
Copyright © 1985 by The Tundra Times

This is the first concrete thing I've seen of somebody really come in here and talking to people about it. I think when you leave here, I think whoever came to this meeting here will understand it so much better. (*Andrew Gronholdt, Sand Point*)

> I think that the fact that these hearings are being held not by a government agency, not by the State of Alaska, not by the United States of America, but these hearings are being held independent on an international level is very significant. (*Don Wright, Fairbanks*)

This 1991 is going to be something happening right there. We are told before that, we are notified and we are requested to put our voice in before that time comes ahead of time. We really don't know because 1991 there will be the voices in some places, a lot of places, just the voices. We are getting old and we all know that old peoples never stays up forever, but their voice and their stories in the books is always stay in front of the young peoples and I am glad the gentleman here. He came around and goes over to the villages and requests for our voice to put the brace of what the Eskimo likes. (*George O. Cleveland, Kobuk*)

> This Review Commission that you are doing, this is what our state should have done, or our people should have done twenty years ago when we were in the process of passing ANCSA. (*John Wuliya, Savoonga*)

I was not planning on testifying today, but hearing all the concerns of my people I decided to. (*Linda Tungiyan, Gambell*)

> People ought to be asked and talked to like we are doing now with interpreters. There are a lot of people with not enough education to understand all of the English language and this is a good thing that has happened to us tonight. I hope people will find out from this hearing about the people's feelings. (*Art Douglas, Ambler*)

I would like to thank you on behalf of the City of Barrow for coming here and hearing testimony from concerned citizens, and I know it has brought out a lot of issues that have been in people's minds all these years, and I think it will be very interesting to read your report, and I think with all the information that you've gathered also would be very educational as much as it has been during the hearing here. Thank you very much. (*Marie Adams, Barrow*)

Her name is Doris Uglowook and she was originally born over in Siberia, but she hardly remembered her days over there and she has spent all of her time here, and she is proud to be an American, is what she said. Basically, what she was saying is that she has never testified or spoke in front of anybody before, but she did so today hoping that her testimony today will help the future generation of young people to come and to keep the land. (*Doris Uglowook, Gambell*) [Translated by Branson Tungiyan]

> It should have been, like I said, it should have been undertaken by twelve regional corporations with X amount of dollars, for this type of testimony should have been long taken care of. (*Jim Wilson, Nondalton*)

This is the first time I ever had the chance to ask questions about my regional corporation and my village corporation. I would like to thank you for the opportunity to voice my opinion. At least I know somebody is listening. (*Mike Trevory, Newhalen*)

> The most I know about 1991 is what I've heard here today, on selling your stock and losing your rights. (*Vern Jensen, Pedro Bay*)

Although I feel very nervous at this moment and I know that, if my parents saw me talking here they'd feel a little shame, and I think that's a Yup'ik trait. But I feel that I should take this privilege to speak now or not be heard when 1991 comes. (*Abby Augustine, Emmonak*)

> I think the Inuit Circumpolar Conference and the World Council of Indigenous Peoples have set up a good way to do it, especially by bringing yourself in and others who are outside the Alaskan situation, but yet understand what's going on here, to some degree, because of the similarities with Canada, to do this examination, and I think that by the time you produce your report, which I am very interested in receiving and reading, will give the people who are concerned with these issues a chance to perhaps get something done in a way that will meet the needs of the people and be politically viable and so on. (*Arnold Brower, Jr., Barrow*)

Judge Berger, on behalf of Unit 4 villages I thank you for being here, your associate, your workers here, and I know that it's the first time unit village is speaking out for their rights, and I'm happy. (*Charlie James, Akiachak*)

*Along
the Yukon River*

Yukon fish camp

Emmonak hearing

I would like to thank this commission for giving me this opportunity to share my thoughts with my people. (*Robert A. Edwardsen, Barrow*)

It is through these meetings that we hold in our villages that we all teach each other and learn from each other. That is the only way we have to try and carry on our tradition and our culture, our Native way of life. (*Axel Johnson, Emmonak*)

But coming to the meeting here, now I can understand a little. Little by little. (*Mack Kvasnikoff, English Bay*)

This is the best way of you having somebody come in and from every villages and have meeting among ourself. (*Kilbourne George, Stevens Village*)

This is working together. . . . (*Pat Gregory, Unalaska*)

Something has to be done about it. I'm glad somebody's listening to the people. (*Herman Morgan, Aniak*)

Medina Flynn, Tununak

Stevens Village

I'm glad now that I'm sitting here talking to you and I'm thanking Mr. Berger for letting us say our say-so. We have the right to say what's right for us. (*Sophie Zaukar, Chauthbaluk*)

> Mr. Berger's Commission here has taken testimony from all walks of life and all different nations. (*Glenn Fredericks, Anchorage and Sleetmute*)

I feel that the commission is a valuable tool. It's reaching out to people that have not been allowed to be heard from. (*Derenty Tabios, Port Graham*)

Sharon Kozevenikoff and Hilda Red Fox, Emmonak

I am really happy hearing the different people from the different places in this region come out here and voice their personal opinions and addressing how they feel about ANCSA, how they feel about land and the subsistence way of life. So, I thought I need to come up here and mostly address the things that I feel. (*Marie Schwind, Kotzebue*)

> I would like to express my gratitude for your being here and all the hard work that you have done throughout the state of Alaska as far as asking viewpoints as to how ANCSA has affected our lives and subsistence and the others. (*Bobby Curtis, Kotzebue*)

It's good to have somebody else come down here and see our . . . what we have to say about this Alaska Native Claims Settlement. Thank you. (*Lillian Lane, Point Hope*)

> We are the parents, the old peoples to put our voice in to those whom put the law in that 1971. It don't take a few words of a few voice. I am glad that we are requested to put our voice in that matter. (*George O. Cleveland, Kobuk*)

He thought that he was always happy to see when the communities meet like this when something important arises. (*Jimmie Toolie, Gambell*) [Translated by Branson Tungiyan]

Five /

A NEW DIRECTION:

THE USES OF HISTORY

We want to continue to have the right and to enjoy the right to continue to
be Alaska Natives, to be Alaska Indians, Alaska Eskimos, to be Aleuts. We
want to continue to maintain our tribal identity. *(John Borbridge, Jr., Juneau)*

United States policy toward Native Americans has always
incorporated two contradictory ideas. On the one hand, the
federal government has worked steadily toward their assimilation, and we have seen how a series of legislative measures
systematically undermined the integrity of the Indian tribes and
divided extensive tracts of Indian land into individually owned
units. ANCSA exemplifies this policy.

From the beginning, however, there has been another tendency in United States policy—explicit recognition of the fact
that Native governments have a distinct place under the Constitution, together with the affirmation of communal land tenure.
That great conservative, Chief Justice John Marshall, powerfully
articulated this policy during the nineteenth century, and both
Congress and the executive branch have espoused it from time
to time since then. Despite ANCSA, this policy has gained
strength in recent years. This policy offers possibilities for the
solution of the problems that ANCSA has created.

The Thirteen Colonies and the New Republic

For many years, England left it to each of the Thirteen Colonies to decide for itself how best to deal with the Native inhabitants of the New World. At the end of the French and Indian
War, however, the government of King George III issued the
Royal Proclamation of 1763: it established a boundary between
the colonies and Indian lands and encouraged colonists to settle

east of the Appalachian Mountains. The boundary created a new concept: Indian Country, a territory that, in general, lay west of the Appalachians and was reserved for the Indians. Officials in the colonies were forbidden to grant lands or even to permit surveys in Indian Country. Whites who had settled in Indian Country were ordered to leave it.

After the War of Independence, the newly constituted United States of America developed its own policy for dealing with the original inhabitants, who still occupied the greater part of the continent. This concern preoccupied the new republic for a century. Treaties were made with the Indians, but the Indians did not always regard those who signed the treaties on their behalf as their true representatives. In December 1786, a confederacy of the Iroquois, Huron, Wyandotte, Delaware, Shawnee, Ottawa, Chippewa, and Cherokee Indians sent a letter to the "Brethren of the United States of America." It said:

> All treaties carried on with the United States, on our part, should be with the general voice of the whole confederacy, and carried on in the most open manner without any restraint on either side; and especially as land matters are often the subject of our councils with you, a matter of the greatest importance and of great concern to us, in this case we hold it indispensably necessary that any cession of our lands should be made in the most public manner, and by the united voice of the confederacy.

Despite the generally restrained tone, a note of indignation crept in. "You have managed everything respecting us your own way. You kindled our council fires where you thought proper, without consulting us, at which you held separate treaties and have entirely neglected our plan of having a general conference with the different nations of the confederacy." At the hearings I held throughout Alaska, I heard the same complaint.

> The U.S. government ignored the mere existence of our tribal governments and ignored proper procedure of having an official representation from the tribal government viewpoint. . . . The federal government should have dealt with the tribal governments

rather than the individual activists at that time. *(Sam George, Akia-chak)*

If anybody is to represent a Native Fort Yukon Native village council, he must have a resolution by the Native council or a letter from the chief. And I guarantee you, none of these negotiators, or those who negotiated the Native land claims, had a piece of paper saying they were to represent the Fort Yukon Native council, because they didn't have a resolution or a letter from the chief. *(Jonathon Solomon, Fort Yukon)*

Many Alaska Natives simply do not accept ANCSA because it was, they believe, imposed on them by Congress. They think now that their traditional tribal governments were the only appropriate bodies to make these decisions, and Congress never consulted with the tribal governments.

The letter from the Indian confederacy mentioned above reached Congress early in 1787. In July, Congress passed an ordinance for the organization of the Northwest Territory (lands beyond the Ohio River), which included this provision:

> The utmost good faith shall always be observed towards the Indi-ans, their lands and property shall never be taken from them without their consent; and in their property, rights and liberty, they never shall be invaded or disturbed, unless in just and lawful wars authorized by Congress; but laws founded in justice and humanity shall from time to time be made, for preventing wrongs being done to them, and for preserving peace and friendship with them.

When, in 1789, the founding fathers of the United States wrote the Constitution, they lodged in Congress the supreme power to deal with the Indians. Under the Commerce Clause, the Consti-tution empowers Congress

> To regulate Commerce with foreign Nations, and among the several States, and with the Indian Tribes.

Gradually, Congress has assumed powers over Indian affairs that are, to a great extent, unqualified.

Congress passed the first Indian Non-Intercourse Act in 1790 to avoid conflict on the frontier by protecting Indians from the sharp practices of White traders. The act provided and still provides that no one may negotiate or enter into agreements with the Indians without first obtaining federal consent. These measures hardly impeded the westward movement of White settlers, who were then pushing into the Northwest Territory, steadily encroaching on Indian lands. Armed clashes occurred. War with the Indians followed in 1790 and 1791, and the United States Army was beaten back. Then in August 1794, the army defeated the Indians at the Battle of Fallen Timbers, and they were forced to surrender practically all of what is now Ohio and much of Indiana.

Farther south and southeast, settlers and state militias were launching attacks upon the Indian peoples there to drive them off their lands. The Indians, led by the Creeks under Alexander McGillivray, fought back. President Washington, already engaged in an Indian war in the northwest, offered to negotiate a settlement with them.

Washington invited Alexander McGillivray to meet him in New York, then capital of the republic. McGillivray (son of an Indian mother and a Scottish father) and some thirty Indian leaders traveled northward in a splendid procession to meet Washington face to face and to sign the Treaty of New York in 1790. President Washington, Secretary of State Jefferson, and Secretary of War Knox signed the treaty personally. McGillivray and twenty-three other Creek leaders added their signatures. The Chief Justice of the State of New York and the Mayor of New York signed as witnesses.

The treaty provided that if any citizen of the United States settled on Creek land without Creek permission, he forfeited the protection of the United States. Entry into Creek territory could be made only with the display of a valid passport. The United States acknowledged the Creeks' right of self-government and provided guarantees for their land.

Like the Creeks, Alaska Natives want to govern themselves, and they also insist on guarantees for their land. It is easy to see a continuity, a coherence, a connectedness in these demands extending in an unbroken line from before Alexander McGillivray's time to the present.

The idea of Native self-government persisted throughout the early years of the Republic. When Jefferson was negotiating the Louisiana Purchase, he drafted an amendment to the Constitution to provide for the incorporation of Louisiana into the Union; it provided that "the rights of occupancy in the soil and of self-government are confirmed to the Indian inhabitants as they now exist." Virtually all of the new territory, except for what is now the state of Louisiana, was to be reserved for the Indians. Jefferson's proposal reflected common ideas of the time about the rights of Native nations. It fell to John Marshall to integrate these ideas into American federalism.

The Courts

In the 1820s and 1830s, Chief Justice Marshall undertook to describe the nature of United States sovereignty, Indian self-government, and Indian title. Marshall accepted the legitimacy of Native sovereignty, Native institutions, and Native title, and he wove them into the American polity. Ever since then, Marshall's analysis of the question has served as the basis for the assertion of Native claims, not only in the United States, but throughout the Western world.

Marshall regarded land and sovereignty as the two vital elements in Indian rights. The assumption of sovereignty by the United States did not extinguish Indian title nor did it deny tribal sovereignty. Nevertheless, in 1828, the Georgia State Assembly annexed the lands of the Cherokee Nation. It established state courts, placed police on Cherokee land, and it annulled all tribal laws and imprisoned tribal officials. When a Cherokee, George Corn Tassels, was indicted for murder of another Cherokee, the state superior court held that the Georgia courts, not the Cherokee tribal courts, had jurisdiction, on the ground that savages can have no lawful government. An appeal was taken to the Supreme Court, but the state assembly had Corn Tassels executed at once. The Cherokees asked the Supreme Court to grant an injunction to stop Georgia enforcing its laws in Cherokee lands.

Under Article III of the Constitution, the Supreme Court only had original jurisdiction to hear "controversies between two or more states; and between a state or the citizens thereof and foreign states, citizens or subjects." The Cherokee Nation was not a state of the Union. Was it a foreign state? Marshall said it was not, and the court declined to hear the case. But if the Cherokee Nation was not a foreign state, what was it? Marshall concluded that Indian tribes are "domestic, dependent nations":

Though the Indians are acknowledged to have an unquestionable, and heretofore, unquestioned right to the lands they occupy, until that right shall be extinguished by a voluntary cession to our government; yet it may well be doubted whether those tribes which reside within the acknowledged boundaries of the United States can, with strict accuracy, be denominated foreign nations. They occupy a territory to which we assert a title independent of their will, which must take effect in point of possession when their right of possession ceases. Meanwhile they are in a state of pupillage. Their relation to the United States resembles that of a ward to his guardian.

Soon the Cherokees brought another case that the court was bound to hear on its merits, *Worcester v. Georgia.* Georgia had imprisoned Samuel Worcester, a New England missionary, for entering former Cherokee territory without a permit from the state. Worcester asked the Supreme Court for a writ of habeas corpus. Marshall returned to the question: By what right did the United States take Indian lands? In a famous passage, Marshall began with speculations about the rule of discovery under which Europeans had laid claim to the New World:

America, separated from Europe by a wide ocean, was inhabited by a distinct people, divided into separate nations, independent of each other and of the rest of the world, having institutions of their own, and governing themselves by their own laws. It is difficult to comprehend the proposition that the inhabitants of either quarter of the globe could have rightful original claims of dominion over the inhabitants of the other, or over the lands they occupied; or that the discovery of either by the other should give the discoverer rights in the country discovered which annulled the preexisting rights of its ancient possessors.

The Europeans, he said, had found America

in possession of a people who had made small progress in agriculture or manufactures, and whose general employment was war,
hunting and fishing. Did these adventurers, by sailing along the
coast and occasionally landing on it, acquire for the several governments to whom they belonged, or by whom they were commissioned, a rightful property in the soil from the Atlantic to the
Pacific; or rightful dominion over the numerous people who occupied it? Or has nature, or the great Creator of all things, conferred
these rights over hunters and fishermen, on agriculturalists and
manufacturers?

Marshall was skeptical, but he was also a practical man. He
answered the question in these words:

But power, war, conquest, give rights, which after possession, are
conceded by the world; and which can never be controverted by
those on whom they descend. We proceed, then, to the actual state
of things, having glanced at their origin, because holding it in our
recollection might shed some light on existing pretensions.

Marshall considered that the rights of the Indians survived,
that European discovery had not extinguished them. Speaking
for the court, Marshall held that Georgia's laws were "repugnant
to the Constitution, laws and treaties of the United States," and
they did not apply to the Cherokee:

The Indian nations had always been considered as distinct, independent political communities, retaining their original natural
rights, as the undisputed possessors of the soil, from time immemorial, with the single exception of that imposed by irresistible
power, which excluded them from intercourse with any other European potentate than the first discoverer of the coast of the particular
region claimed; and this was a restriction which those European
potentates imposed on themselves, as well as on the Indians. The
very term "nation," so generally applied to them, means "a people
distinct from others." . . . The words "treaty" and "nation" are
words of our own language, selected in our diplomatic and legisla-

tive proceedings, by ourselves, having each a definite and well understood meaning. We have applied them to Indians, as we have applied them to the other nations of the earth.

Andrew Jackson was President in 1832, when the Supreme Court decided *Worcester v. Georgia.* Jackson did not think that the Indians could exist within independent enclaves inside the United States, and he did not accept the Supreme Court's judgment. "John Marshall has made his judgment," Jackson is supposed to have said, "now let him enforce it." The statement may be apocryphal, but it represents Jackson's view of the matter. Under President Jackson and his successor, Martin Van Buren, many Indian tribes were driven hundreds of miles to the west, leaving their fertile homelands in the eastern United States open to White settlement.

Do these actions mean that Marshall's judgments, acclaimed throughout the Western world, mean nothing in United States constitutional history? Are they nothing more than good theoretical stuff, of no practical use? No, I believe Marshall's judgments hold the key we need to unlock the riddle of ANCSA. Native governments have always been part of the American political system, not as "foreign" nations, but as "domestic, dependent nations."

Once the tribes had been removed to the West, even Jackson was prepared to concede their right to live autonomously on their own lands. Implicit in the autonomy of the western Indian nations was the idea of Indian Country, to the west of existing White settlements, where Indians could live free from White control. From the Jacksonian era until today, the United States has recognized the domestic sovereignty of Indian tribes. Although Indian Country has steadily diminished, there the Indians have governed themselves on their own land.

President Jackson's refusal to enforce Marshall's judgment demonstrated the vulnerability of Indian tribes. Events on the ground, not theories of law, no matter how carefully crafted, have often been the true determinants of Indian rights. Yet, even when tribes were forcibly being removed to the West, no one suggested that the physical power to remove them implied a legal power to deny them self-government on their own lands. On the reservations, they were to govern themselves.

In 1871, Congress ceased to make treaties with the Indians and approved a rider to an appropriations bill that stated that no Indian tribe should any longer be "acknowledged or recognized as an independent tribe or power with whom the United States may contract by treaty." Thereafter, Congress dealt with Indian tribes by legislation, executive order, or agreement.

In 1883, the Supreme Court held that federal laws against murder did not apply to crimes between Indians on their reservations, and it remanded to his tribe an Indian defendant to be treated according to tribal custom and law. This led Congress, in 1885, to pass the Major Crimes Act, which extended federal jurisdiction to Indian reservations. The federal government hired Indians to serve as police officers and judges of new federally controlled courts to deal with Indian offenses on reservations. They exercised jurisdiction over some reservations, establishing a power structure that rivaled traditional forms of tribal governance. Federal law now extended into Indian Country. During this period, federal authorities began to keep Indian children for years in boarding schools to remove them from the influence of their parents and tribes. They banned virtually everything that was Indian, including dress, language, and religious practices. This policy continued into our own times, both in the Lower 48 and in Alaska.

As long as Native Americans still occupied lands beyond the frontier of White settlement, the federal authorities acknowledged their legal and constitutional position: they occupied Indian Country that was geographically distinct and, for a time, they were able to defend it. But when White settlement gradually overcame them, reducing the Native population to remnants living within enclaves on reservations dependent on federal support, the federal authorities found it easier to reject the idea that the Indians should enjoy a distinct and quite special constitutional status. Liberal democracy, in its triumph, no longer regarded Native Americans as one of the great founding elements of the nation; it now considered the Indians should have no rights beyond those enjoyed by other minorities.

The General Allotment Act of 1887 applied throughout the United States, and it firmly rejected tribal ownership of land in the expectation of changing the Indians into farmers. When they had severed their links with the tribe, they would become citizens. This philosophy of assimilation, which led the federal government to reject tribal government, the Native economy, and Native cultures, not only inspired the General Allotment Act but also constitutes the ideological foundation of ANCSA. As Fred Paul, a Tlingit lawyer told me, "Natives would be brought into the twentieth century screaming and hollering." Tribal governments in Alaska are in the same peril in which tribal governments found themselves after the General Allotment Act: they do not hold title to ancestral lands, which have been deeded to private corporations composed of individual shareholders. Although at present individual shares are restricted, when restrictions are lifted, the shares will certainly be sold and the land lost.

The Indian Reorganization Act and Self-Determination

With the first administration of President Franklin Delano Roosevelt, a new era for Native Americans began. John Collier, architect of the Indian New Deal, served as Commissioner of Indian Affairs from 1933 until 1945; he had been deeply influenced by the communal values he had observed in the Pueblo Indian societies of the southwestern United States. In devising a new Indian policy, he tried in many ways to enhance tribal values and to secure tribal lands. In 1934, on Collier's initiative, Congress passed the Indian Reorganization Act.

> To conserve and develop Indian lands and resources; to extend to Indians the right to form business and other organizations; to establish a credit system for Indians; [and] to grant certain rights of home rule to Indians.

The Indian Reorganization Act (IRA) ended further dismemberment of reservation lands. Indeed, the federal government began to buy land to replace lands lost to reservations after 1887. The act affirmed the status of tribal governments as distinct from federal, state, and local governments, and it enabled Native communities to adopt a constitution to reconstruct their tribal governments. Once they had adopted a constitution, they could obtain a federal charter to establish tribal business corporations. Alaska Natives often refer to any tribal government as an IRA government.

The IRA governments did not supplant the many forms of traditional Native governments; they served as a federal overlay. The act applied to Indian tribes "residing on reservations." Few Alaska Natives lived on reservations, so, in 1936, Congress amended the act to enable Alaska Native "groups . . . not heretofore recognized as bands or tribes" to reorganize themselves for governmental and business purposes on the basis of "a common bond of occupation, or association, or residence within a well-defined neighborhood, community or rural district."

The Indian New Deal had far-reaching effects. Tribal governments in the Lower 48 today are autonomous political bodies, capable of maintaining themselves against the power of the states as a third sovereignty. For the first time, Congress had enacted legislation based on Marshall's conception of the relation of Indian nations to the federal government. The act inaugurated a change in federal policies and legislation that has culminated in laws favorable to self-determination during the last decade.

This new line of policy did not proceed, however, without interruption. Senator Arthur V. Watkins, chairman of the Senate subcommittee on Indian Affairs, believed that the Indians' status as wards of the federal government should be ended. He proclaimed: "I see the following words, emblazoned in letters of fire above the heads of Indians—THESE PEOPLE SHALL BE FREE!" His policy of termination contemplated the breaking up of the tribes and foresaw a future for Native Americans as industrial workers in the cities.

In 1953, Congress passed House Concurrent Resolution 108, which declared that it was the

> sense of Congress that, at the earliest possible time, all of the Indian Tribes . . . should be freed from Federal supervision and control and from all disabilities and limitations specifically applicable to Indians.

The resolution passed both houses of Congress without opposition. As one by one tribes were chosen for termination, federal statutes severed the special relation that had existed between the federal government and the tribes chosen for termination. Federal programs both to tribes and to individual Indians were discontinued. Today, the principal legacy of the termination policy is Public Law 280, the first federal law of general application to authorize certain states to assume civil and criminal jurisdiction over Indian Country. Public Law 280, where it is in force, overlays tribal law and tribal courts with state law and state courts. This law was extended to Alaska in 1958.

Termination policy was discredited within less than a decade; within two decades, the restoration of terminated tribes was underway. Like the allotment policy, termination had not worked. Peter McDonald, chairman of the Navaho tribe, said:

> In the 1950s, they tried to turn us into workers for industrial America. They relocated us to the cities. They decided we must become factory hands. They shipped hundreds of thousands of us off the reservation. They terminated some tribes, the program was a disaster. It destroyed nearly half of a generation, and the last monument to that effort is the existence of dozens of small Indian ghettos, pockets of misery, unemployment, crime and alcoholism in major urban centers.

The adamant refusal of Indians to agree with the policy, and changing public attitudes, limited its implementation. During President Kennedy's Administration, Secretary of the Interior Stewart Udall announced that House Concurrent Resolution 108 had "died with the 83rd Congress," and every administration since 1960 has continued to reject it. Indeed, Congress has passed legislation to restore tribal status to one tribe of terminated Indians after another.

In 1973, Congress reestablished the Menominee tribe and returned their land to trust status under a unique trust agreement which reestablished tribal and federal jurisdiction and again made the tribe and its members eligible for federal services. The Menominees have adopted a new constitution, providing for a tribal legislature and a tribal court. Under the trust agreement, the tribe makes most decisions and delivers most services under contract with federal agencies.

Ada Deer, a leader in achieving the restoration of tribal status to the Menominees, told my commission:

One of the continuing themes that the majority culture never seems to hear is that Indians want to be Indians. Indians want to retain culture, want to retain land, and want to live as Indians live. Now, of course, this does vary from tribe to tribe and from region to region, but I really want to emphasize that, despite many policies of the federal government over the years, from removal to putting people on reservations, to allotment, to assimilation, the continuing wish and desire of Indian people is to remain Indian, and this never seems to get across.

The Resurgence of Tribal Government

The place of Native tribal institutions within the American federal system, originally asserted by John Marshall, has been reaffirmed by Congress, by executive decisions, and by the judiciary. In 1968, Congress enacted the Indian Civil Rights Act. It amended Public Law 280 to require tribal consent for all future acquisition by states of jurisdiction over Indian Country, and it also authorized the federal government to take back jurisdiction over Indian Country if a state requested it. The act requires tribal governments and tribal courts to adhere to the principles of the Bill of Rights.

In President Nixon's message to Congress in 1970, he provided a blueprint for Native self-determination in one of the most powerful statements any president has made on Indian affairs:

> The time has come to break decisively with the past and to create the conditions for a new era in which the Indian future is determined by Indian acts and Indian decisions. . . .
>
> This policy of forced termination is wrong, in my judgment. . . .
>
> This . . . must be the goal of any new national policy toward the Indian people: to strengthen the Indian's sense of autonomy without threatening his sense of community. We must assure the Indian that he can assume control of his own life without being separated involuntarily from the tribal group. And we must make it clear that Indians can become independent of Federal control without being cut off from Federal concern and Federal support. . . .
>
> Because termination is morally and legally unacceptable, because it produces bad practical results, and because the mere threat

of termination tends to discourage greater self-sufficiency among Indian groups, I am asking the Congress to pass a new Concurrent Resolution which would expressly renounce, repudiate and repeal the termination policy as expressed in House Concurrent Resolution 108 of the 83rd Congress.

In 1975, Congress, in an evident repudiation of Resolution 108, enacted the Indian Self-Determination and Education Assistance Act. This act gives tribes power to contract with the Secretary of the Interior and with the Secretary of Health and Human Services for the creation and implementation of federally funded Indian programs. The two secretaries are now required to contract with the Native tribes. The Indian Child Welfare Act, 1978, explicitly rejected assimilation and the removal of Native children from their homes, and it confirmed a broad jurisdiction of tribal courts over Indian children.

Other legislation passed during the 1970s strengthened and reorganized a revolving federal fund for Indian economic development and provided federal loan guarantees for private-sector loans to support such development. Other legislation improved Indian health-care services and established and funded tribally controlled community colleges. The Indian Tribal Governmental Tax Status Act, 1982, treats tribes as states for certain federal tax purposes. Alaska Native villages have been specifically included in all this legislation as tribes.

President Reagan, in a statement of policy made on January 24, 1983, declared that, in relation to "federally recognized American Indian tribes,"

> The Constitution, treaties, laws, and court decisions have consistently recognized a unique political relationship between Indian tribes and the United States which this Administration pledges to uphold.

In perhaps the most important paragraph, the President said:

> This Administration honors the commitment this nation made in 1970 and 1975 to strengthen tribal governments and lessen federal control over tribal governmental affairs. This Administration is

determined to turn these goals into reality. Our policy is to reaffirm dealing with Indian tribes on a government-to-government basis and to pursue the policy of self-government for Indian tribes without threatening termination.

Existing arrangements for tribal government are not a halfway house on the road to assimilation. Tribal institutions are not regarded as exceptional or transitional. The President's policy statement concludes with this summary:

> This Administration intends to restore tribal governments to their rightful place among the governments of this nation and to enable tribal governments, along with state and local governments, to resume control over their own affairs.

Tribal Government in Alaska

ANCSA came at a time when the idea of tribal government was gaining ground in Congress. Yet, while enacting ANCSA, Congress ignored tribal government, at the very time it had under consideration the Menominees' petition for restoration of their tribal government. The ambivalence of the federal government in pursuit of policies for Native Americans has often been seen in measures taken in Alaska. Some have argued that this is because Alaska Natives are not tribes and that federal policies that benefit Native Americans in the Lower 48 should not be extended to Alaska. Yet a careful examination of Alaska's history reveals that the federal government has treated Alaska Natives and other Native Americans in the same way, both before and after ANCSA.

When in 1867 the United States signed the Treaty of Cession with Russia for the purchase of Alaska, it was a time of transition in American history. The Civil War had just ended, and the reunited nation continued its push to the Pacific Ocean. The last of the Indian wars were just beginning, to be followed by the effective confinement of Indians to reservations and by the undermining of the tribal system and the breakup of tribal lands.

Nevertheless, in 1867, Marshall's concept of the special political status of Native tribes was the basis for treaties that the federal government made with them in the Lower 48. This concept also informed the federal attitude to Alaska Natives under the Treaty of Cession, Article III of which provides for the treatment of the "uncivilized Native tribes" and equates them with the other "aboriginal tribes" of the United States.

> The inhabitants of the ceded territory . . . with the exception of uncivilized Native tribes, shall be admitted to the enjoyment of the rights, advantages and immunities of citizens of the United States. . . . The uncivilized tribes will be subject to such laws and regulations as the United States may, from time to time, adopt with regard to aboriginal tribes of that country.

All Indian tribes in the United States were thought of as "uncivilized" at this time; it is not, therefore, surprising that the treaty employed this usage.

Early federal programs in Alaska focused primarily on the education of Alaska Natives. Beginning in 1885, the federal Bureau of Education established Native village schools, a Native-run reindeer industry, cooperative stores, sawmills, salmon canneries, and other commercial enterprises. Later, the bureau provided medical care. Some 150 reservations were established in Alaska; they ranged in size from a few acres for schools to several thousand acres for reindeer herding or for the preservation of subsistence activities. In 1923, the Solicitor for the Department of the Interior concluded:

> The relations existing between [the Alaska Natives] and the government are very similar and, in many respects, identical with those which have long existed between the government and the aboriginal people residing within the territorial limits of the United States.

In 1931, the Bureau of Indian Affairs took over the administration of federal programs for Alaska Natives. When in 1932 Representative Edgar Howard, chairman of the House Committee on Indian Affairs, requested information from the Secretary of the Interior on "the status of the Indian Tribes in Alaska," the Solicitor for the Department of the Interior replied:

It is clear that no distinction has been or can be made between the Indians and other natives of Alaska so far as the laws and relations of the United States are concerned whether the Eskimos and other Natives are of Indian origin or not as they are all wards of the Nation, and their status is in material respects similar to that of the Indians of the United States.

The Alaska Reorganization Act of May 1, 1936, extended to Alaska additional provisions of the Indian Reorganization Act to offer a new form of federal protection to Alaska Natives "who in the past," according to Commissioner of Indian Affairs John Collier, "have seen their land rights almost universally disregarded, their fishing rights increasingly invaded, and their economic situation grow each year more desperate." Insofar as federal recognition of tribal sovereignty is concerned, this act removed the last significant difference (if, indeed, there had been any) between the legal status of American Indians and that of Alaska Natives. The act also permitted the Secretary of the Interior to designate new Indian reservations in Alaska. Furthermore, waters adjacent to reserved land could be reserved for the exclusive use of the Natives occupying the reservation.

Secretary of the Interior Harold Ickes favored the establishment of reservations in Alaska. He issued a memorandum on July 27, 1945, in which he referred to the successful reservation of the Tsimshian Indians at Metlakatla:

[Without] government loans or subsidies, they have built, on the uninhabited island reserved to them by act of Congress, one of the model communities of the Western Hemisphere. This municipality operates, profitably, a power plant, saw mill, fish traps and one of the most modern canneries in Alaska. . . . There is no reason why our own native Indians of Alaska should not do as well as these Metlakatlan immigrants from British Columbia, once they have some assurance that the land on which they live belongs to them and that the developments and improvements which they undertake upon that land will accrue to the benefit of themselves and their posterity. They will not be degraded nor endanger their citizenship thereby. Improvement in their economic status will help them and the whole territory of Alaska.

Despite Ickes's approval of it, the IRA system and reservations were never fully implemented in Alaska. Alaska Governor Ernest Gruening maintained that creation of reservations for Alaska Natives was "wholly destructive," a view endorsed by most non-Native Alaskans. There was also opposition to it in Congress. Representative Henry Jackson from Washington, speaking in Alaska, commented:

> It is high time to stop treating the Indians as second-class citizens. Indians ought to be treated just as other citizens and assimilated into our population.

John Hope, chairman of the Tlingit and Haida Central Council and a member of the board of Sealaska, urged me to visit Metlakatla, the only Indian reservation remaining after 1971 in Alaska. The people there had rejected ANCSA, and their leaders lobbied in Washington, D.C., against their being included in it. I did visit Metlakatla, and at the hearing there the people told me they believe they had been right to stay out of ANCSA.

> I believe that now, looking at some of the results of the settlement, I still strongly believe that we made the right decision at that time. *(Casey Nelson, Metlakatla)*

> The council has always been aware of the reservation status that it had received through the [Royal] Proclamation that was given [in 1763]. And they're also aware of the [General] Allotment Act . . . whereby the government did primarily the same thing they're doing here in 1991, giving title to the land. And they're aware of the consequences that happened . . . where tribes, where reservations, were broken up by Natives and non-Natives, to the point where they were nicknamed the checkerboard reservations. And these things were things that the council had heavy on their minds. *(Stan Patterson, Metlakatla)*

> We didn't want any other land. We didn't want to participate because if we did . . . they said, if you participate, and each one of you gets so many thousand dollars from the oil land, you'll lose the island. Everybody can come and join you. They can join you

and that is it. And we—from our past experience, we know that all these years we've lived pretty well off this island. Our men don't have to beg anybody to fish any place. *(John Smith, Metlakatla)*

In terms of economic activity and of local employment, Metlakatla, an Indian reservation, has been more successful than any village corporation established by ANCSA that I have visited.

We have a background of a hundred years of business involvement. We are the oldest people in the canned-salmon industry, anywhere, in continuous operation. People started canning fish in Canada, long before they move here. *(Ira Booth, Metlakatla)*

The importance of Metlakatla in the present context is that here is an Alaska Native village that does not face the prospect of losing its ancestral lands. The people of Metlakatla have managed to stay within the stream of United States policy that recognizes tribal government and tribal ownership. They have a thriving fishing industry, a cannery, a logging operation, and a sawmill. Moreover, none of these economic ventures will place the future of the community itself at risk.

The idea that Alaska Natives are distinct from other Native Americans is unacceptable. To say that the Tsimshian Indians of Metlakatla are somehow different from the Tlingits and Haidas, who live on the same coast, or that they are somehow different from the rest of Alaska's Native populations, is nonsense. The plain fact is that Metlakatla has kept its land under tribal ownership. No other Native village in Alaska was allowed to do that, and now all of these other villages are threatened by the loss of their lands.

The question here is not one of reservations or no reservations. The vital fact about the village of Metlakatla is that the land is under tribal ownership, under the jurisdiction of a Native government, not that it is a reservation. It is Indian Country. No case can be made, on the strength of Alaska's history, that only one village—and no others—should have the right to institutions that protect Native land under Native ownership.

ANCSA departed from official United States policy that has

long recognized tribal governments and tribal lands. Alaska Natives have a rendezvous with history. John Marshall's judgments speak to the dilemma that ANCSA poses in Alaska today. Alaska Natives must have institutions and forms of land tenure that reflect Native cultural imperatives. This requires the exercise of Native sovereignty.

Six

NATIVE SOVEREIGNTY

IN ALASKA

Tribal government has existed since time immemorial. It was governing here in 1492, at the time when Columbus supposedly discovered America. The elders say, "Reestablish your own governments, practice self-determination. We must understand the ways of the majority, but we must not forget who we are." *(Willie Kasayulie, Akiachak)*

Chefornak is a village of two hundred Eskimos, on the edge of the Bering Sea. I arrived on the day the people had met to consider the adoption of a written tribal constitution. Discussion went on in Yup'ik for an afternoon. Their sense that a tribal government is best for them was manifest, for they consider that neither a municipal form of government nor a corporation suits their needs. They want Native political institutions. They are talking about sovereignty.

ANCSA did not address the issue of Native sovereignty. Byron Mallott, past president of the Alaska Federation of Natives, Inc., and president of Sealaska Corporation, said:

The business of sovereignty . . . was left on the table. . . . If, at 1991, these institutions [the corporations] don't do what Native people want them to do, we will have lost sovereignty as a practical effect of ANCSA. That is, we may still exist as Indian people, we may still have the values, we may still have aspirations, we may still maintain a unique identity, but the institutions that were created, and the monetary and land settlements that were established, will have reached a point wherein Native people will have lost a very incredible kind of opportunity. And, in my judgment, that would be a very, very severe blow to the aspirations of Native people.

Charlie Johnson, president of the Alaska Federation of Natives, Inc., said that Alaska Natives are not just citizens of the United

States, but distinct peoples who require their own institutions. He felt the corporations are a sufficient expression of the Natives' desire for their own institutions. On the other hand, Sheldon Katchatag, president of the United Tribes of Alaska, thinks that Native institutions should be political, that is, they must have the authority to make laws, an authority derived from the limited sovereignty possessed by tribal governments as domestic dependent nations.

What Is Native Sovereignty?

Before the Europeans came, the Native peoples of the Americas governed themselves. Native sovereignty preceded that of the Thirteen Colonies and of the United States and it derives from a different people. The Native peoples of the New World have always thought of themselves as sovereign peoples, and so did the Spanish scholar Francisco de Vitoria and other European scholars of his time.

> [The Indians] were told that Columbus discovered America and here is how you are going to live. If a single Native can speak English at that time, he would reply, "No, no, no! We are the first Americans. Therefore, here's how you'll live in our country." Our people have one perpetual goal—self-determination, freedom, and peace. *(Roger Silook, Gambell)*

But the European discoverers, their descendants, and the nations they founded, including the United States, imposed their overlordship on the peoples of the New World. The Europeans came, and they claimed the land. No one has ever advanced a sound legal theory to justify the taking of Native land from the Natives of the New World, whether by the Spanish, the Portuguese, the French, the English, the Dutch, the Americans, or—in Alaska—by the Russians.

Whereas, in Latin America, the Spanish and Portuguese suggested the advance of civilization and the spread of Christianity as justification for the appropriation of Native lands, in North America the rule of discovery served as justification. Certain European powers claimed by virtue of discovery the exclusive right to purchase land from its original inhabitants. The rule of discovery depends upon the concept of Native sovereignty: only if the original inhabitants had the right to sell their land could the discoverer exercise his right to purchase it. The only way to justify a transfer of title to the land was to accept the concept of Native sovereignty and the Natives' capacity to dispose of their own lands.

It was British policy to acknowledge Indian title, then to treat for it, as with any other sovereign power. The British process of treaty-making by imperial authority illustrates how comprehensively European and colonial governments accepted and acted on the concept of aboriginal sovereignty. For the Europeans, Native sovereignty was a practical, not a conceptual, problem because for many years after White settlement began, the Native Americans had the military power and the populations to defend their lands. Treaties were made, land was ceded, and trade began. Meantime, the Indians continued to govern themselves on their unsurrendered lands. As the Native peoples of North America were progressively overwhelmed, the importance of international legal principles receded in the European mind. Today, however, these principles of international law are reemerging along with the concept of Native sovereignty.

Many Alaskans and other Americans consider sovereignty to be an absolute—a misconception and a stubborn one. The nation-states of the eighteenth century believed in an absolute, unified sovereignty; that is, they believed that sovereign power could reside in only one national government. For them, sovereignty was one and indivisible. The founding fathers of the United States rejected this and, according to some authorities, they borrowed and popularized the idea of a divided sovereignty from the Iroquois Confederacy, a radical notion at the time. In this concept, sovereignty flows from the people, and is delegated to both federal and state governments.

Anthropologists agree that even the smallest bands of hunters and gatherers have had political processes of some kind to govern themselves. Some Native societies, such as the Iroquois, had a formal system of government and even sophisticated political federations of tribes. Before and after contact, Native peoples of the New World governed themselves according to a variety of political systems, but, whatever the form of their political institutions, they were acknowledged to be sovereign as distinct peoples. They had mechanisms for the identification of territorial boundaries, the maintenance of political autonomy, and the regulation of affairs with other societies. Ancient political systems have adapted to new challenges with new forms. New institutional forms have been introduced and adopted, but decision-making at the village level remains grounded in traditional ways and values.

Neither Russia nor the United States ever conquered Alaska, nor have Alaska Natives ever voluntarily given up or treated to give up their inherent political powers. They have not been absorbed into the mainstream of American society, and their occupation of their ancestral homelands remains unbroken. Sovereignty inheres in the Native people.

Sovereignty derives from the people. . . . Well, we, the people, are still here, and we still have our sovereignty. We can't wait for Washington, D.C., or Juneau. We should start acting like sovereigns. Why can't we pass our own laws? *(Lonnie Strong Hotch, Klukwan)*

Inupiat values . . . traditional councils have these values as backbones. . . . Our Inupiat values are respectable. Our IRA's and the statewide tribes of Alaska are valuable and respectable—our key to survival. *(Virginia Commack, Shungnak)*

The Yup'iks had their own government for many years before the IRA was introduced. Yup'iks had their own instructions from way back, you know. That was government. The IRA has that and that's its jobs. And that whole idea is powerful and can be defined by one word by the White men: sovereignty. *(Mike Albert, Tununak)*

I think that Native people are capable of governing themselves. They always have been and they always will be. *(Margie Johnson, Eyak)*

Sovereignty, the IRA, and ANCSA

In 1936, Congress amended the Indian Reorganization Act to enable Natives in Alaska that have a "common bond of occupation, or association, or residence within a well-defined neighbor-hood, community or rural district" to organize under the act. Some seventy Alaska villages have organized IRA councils under its terms. Many villages that do not have IRA councils are governed by traditional councils. Their recognition by Congress is indisputable: all of these villages, whether governed by IRA councils or by traditional councils, have as much right to be called tribes as any Indian community in the Lower 48.

ANCSA, as a matter of policy, intended to avoid the establish-ment of "permanently racially defined institutions," a policy that some regard as evidence of an intention to terminate tribal sovereignty in Alaska. But the only institutions that ANCSA established are the Native corporations. To carry out ANCSA's policy, Congress provided for the sale of shares in the Native corporations to non-Natives after 1991. This policy is directed against an economic institution, the corporation, not against a political institution, the tribal government. Since Congress enacted ANCSA in 1971, both the executive branch and Con-gress have continued to recognize their special relationship with Alaska Natives, a relationship based on cooperation between the federal government and Alaska Natives as complementary sov-ereigns.

Native governments are not merely organizations to keep Native lands from leaving Native hands. In Alaska, Native governments can also act as local governments, managing the land and passing laws to control activities, especially subsist-ence activities, on them. I think it is obvious that the sovereignty movement in Alaska has arisen in response to the twin crises of land and subsistence. Alaska Natives regard tribal govern-ment as the best means of keeping their lands in Native hands and the best means of defending their own subsistence activities and rights against further encroachments.

So determined are the Native people to keep their land that some communities who live on former reservations have taken or obtained measures to thwart ANCSA. Reservations in exis-tence in 1971 had the option of setting up corporations to select both surface and subsurface rights to the land represented by their former reserves; this exempted them from most of ANCSA's other provisions. Not surprisingly, the villages on large reserves (Venetie, Tetlin, Elim, and St. Lawrence Island) chose to keep their lands, and in every case, they have told me, they consider their choice a wise one, although it meant giving up almost all of ANCSA's cash benefits.

When ANCSA was passed, the people of St. Lawrence Island chooses the whole island instead of cash settlement, with the understanding that the survival of the people was from the land. They understand the land and the waters around it brought the people for thousands of years in which the land was their life—identity —as well as their habitation. They understand the close relationship with the land, the life-giving resources it brought. *(Roger Silook, Gambell)*

When 1971, the Native land claims [act] came into law we had a choice of whether to take the land or take the money. And the people very wisely took the land, and they say, We don't want no part of that money. We'd rather have the land, and that's the way it stands today. And it's up to the people in the tribal council to keep up that tradition of keeping the land as it is, and we call ourselves a sovereign people. And that's the way it should be, because we don't have to ask anybody, we going to hunt on our land or to get timber to build our cabins. We go out and do it without any waste, and we have our own laws that follow, that's been in existence before the White man law came into the village, came into the country. And we still follow that. That's a traditional law. *(Larry Williams, Venetie)*

The other reserves were relatively small; all but one of them, Klukwan, elected to accept ANCSA benefits. Klukwan chose to keep the 893 acres of its former reserve. The IRA village council had signed a mining lease, negotiated before the reservation was abolished, and it claimed a right to the proceeds of the lease, even though ANCSA had conveyed the land to the village corporation. Most of the surface lands around Klukwan were unavailable for selection by the village. In 1976, Congress amended ANCSA to permit Klukwan, Inc., the village corporation, to receive 23,000 acres on Long Island, hundreds of miles from the village, as its entitlement under ANCSA. The legislation required Klukwan, Inc. to convey the 893 acres of the former reserve in fee simple to the IRA village council. Evidently, Congress does not oppose the transfer of ANCSA lands to tribal governments. The federal district court has affirmed the jurisdiction of Klukwan's IRA village council over these lands. They are Indian Country. Nor is this the only case in which land has been transferred from an ANCSA corporation to a tribal government. Two ANCSA corporations on the former Chandalar reserve have transferred all of their lands, 1.8 million acres, to the Venetie tribal government, which has successfully maintained jurisdiction over these lands so far.

The issue of taxing ANCSA lands reveals the vital difference between tribal government and private ownership of ancestral lands. When you consider that, altogether, the Native corporations hold forty-four million acres of private land and that this land constitutes ninety-nine percent of all the private land in the state, it is obvious that treating this land as taxable has a certain artificiality. Almost all land in Alaska is divided among three interests: the federal government, the state, and the Natives. Placing Native-owned lands under private ownership did not alter the proportions of this division, it simply jeopardized the Native peoples' hold on their lands.

There are several reasons why these lands should not be taxed. They are Native ancestral lands, and they should not be treated as private lands just because they are owned by institutions called corporations. Much of the land has no economic value in conventional terms. Moreover, very few of the two hundred Native village corporations are likely to be in a financial position to pay property taxes in any foreseeable future. Yet, profit-making corporations do own this land, a fact that seems to undermine other arguments for not taxing them. The argument for their immunity from taxation is persuasive only if a Native government can claim that immunity.

State-Tribal Relations

Although the federal government has always recognized the sovereignty of Native tribes, the states, including Alaska, have usually been reluctant to do so. I found that Alaska Natives are determined nonetheless to assert their sovereignty. Millie Buck at Gulkana said, "The state is going to have to recognize us as a people." Many others voiced similar convictions:

We got an IRA council before the state came upon the scene. *(Mike Albert, Tununak)*

The tribe has attempted to deal with the State of Alaska, which it has legislative authority to do, on a one-to-one basis, a government-to-government basis, and the state administrations since 1971 have refused to recognize the sovereign status, the tribal status of . . . Venetie. . . . But on the other hand, we have letters from the President of the United States and from the Commissioner of Indian Affairs and the area director that say we definitely are a tribal government. *(Don Wright, Venetie)*

ANCSA, however, attempted to stimulate the formation of state-chartered governments in the villages.

It seems to me, at this point, that the U.S. government and the State of Alaska are just trying to undermine our tribal-government status by creating what they call city governments in all villages throughout Alaska, school districts, and what we call corporations. In every village, that's totally destroying the unity of Native people. *(Sam George, Akiachak)*

Under ANCSA, Section 14(c)(3), each village corporation is required to transfer up to 1,280 acres to a state-chartered local government for village expansion. If there is no state-chartered local government, the state will hold the land in trust until a municipality is formed. These measures have strengthened municipal government in the villages at the expense of tribal government.

We . . . have the 14(c)(3) land reconveyances that is supposed to go to municipality or the state in trust until you form a municipality, if none exists. To me, this is also taking Native lands because this village right here was built with tribal monies and with tribal blood, sweat, and tears, if you want to call it that, after the land claims was passed. Under the land-claims law, you have to turn the core townships into a municipal type of government, or turn it into the state trust until there is one formed at a future date. To me, the village has lost. The Native village of Tyonek IRA council, the tribe, has lost a great asset, or that is by no means settled by this time. But we don't perceive it as the law is just, in trying to take our lands from the tribe. *(Don Standifer, Tyonek)*

ANCSA has no provision for the transfer of land to IRA councils or traditional councils. Most villages want to see this policy reversed or left open for their own determination.

When OPEC escalated world oil prices, Alaska's coffers over-flowed. The state made some of these unprecedented revenues available to state-chartered municipalities, and they began to mobilize resources—manpower, money, land, and laws—to administer many new programs. These programs have recruited many non-Natives into the villages to serve as administrators.

Where a majority of Natives must contend with a substantial non-Native minority, conflicts may be drawn along racial lines and, indeed, the non-Natives may take power. The fact is, state-chartered local government gives non-Natives access to power. There has been a Native majority in Nome for the past twenty years, but Whites have always controlled the city council.

We have . . . Native villages governed by two governments, a Native and a city. And it comes down to: Who is the governing body in that community? Because the city must run by the laws of the state, and anybody can come into a city, based on the laws of the state, and can participate and shape the government. And if what has happened in other places runs true to form, and it never has been an exception, we Native peoples can become outsiders in our villages because values come from other places and are imposed upon us. *(Sheila Aga Theriault, Larsen Bay)*

The most notable exception to this pattern of White dominance of municipal institutions is the North Slope Borough. Here the Inupiat control 88,000 square miles incorporated under state law as a home-rule borough that has the powers of taxation and zoning. Nevertheless, the management of this borough, until now run by Eskimos, could fall into non-Native hands. In 1983, thirty-nine percent of voters in Barrow, the largest village in the borough, were not Inupiat. There was nearly a threefold increase (286 percent) in the number of non-Inupiat who voted in the borough election. As Jimmy Stotts, a former president of the borough assembly, speaking at Barrow, said:

> I myself feel compelled to say that the IRA councils in our area, namely the North Slope of Alaska, are more representative of the Inupiat perspective than the state municipal governments. The reason is very simple: it's simply because membership to the village and regional IRA's is restricted to only Inupiat membership.

Given the inducements of ANCSA and the funneling of state wealth into state-chartered municipal governments, it is astonishing that IRA councils and traditional councils have not faded away entirely. Alaska Natives have not, in general, embraced state-chartered governments. In many parts of the state, Natives see tribal government as the only means by which the crisis of 1991 can be averted. Everywhere I went, the Natives want to take steps now to ensure that their lands remain in Native hands, if the corporations cannot preserve them.

> The only way that I believe that we can salvage the land is by going through the tribal governments. . . . That is why I proposed that the land be separated from the corporations and be given to the tribal governments, because that is where the ultimate authority lies, and that's who the true landowners are. *(Charlie Kairiuak, Chefornak)*

> On the land that's currently in the profit corporation . . . I am all for trying to see it put into . . . tribal councils . . . because I see a lot of corporations failing. And, as of 1991, we're just going to lose it. And we need it, not just for ourselves, but mainly for our children. *(Helen Weiss, Port Lions)*

> The traditional and IRA councils have a big stake in the land because we're using, historically and now, in the present . . . our land. The land is intricately tied to our way of life. . . . We have a lack of governance to the land, and the concern that we have is

to continuously hold on to the land in perpetuity. . . . I hope that
our land will be given back to the traditional and IRA councils.
(Homer Hunter, Scammon Bay)

It is our responsibility to select the land or set of options that
guarantees maximum protection of our lands over time. We need
to lock up our lands tight to make sure that they will be in Native
hands forever, not just for a few years, not just for the short term,
not just for our generation—forever. To achieve this, I don't see
how we can leave them in existing corporations, as the law stands
now. There are too many dangers and too many risks of losing
them. *(Mary Miller, Nome)*

Many Natives described their conviction that tribal councils
should serve as a bulwark against assimilation and the loss of
land. This conviction runs deep.

If we choose to go for IRA, to being Yup'ik, if we choose that, we
will have chosen to make our livelihood from this land any way we
want to. *(Carl Flynn, Tununak)*

We could lose . . . we could lose all the land right now. And the
children that have been born since 1971, I think that . . . to me,
that's the strongest argument . . . for transferring resources to a
tribe, because the children can enroll . . . become enrolled full-
fledged members of a tribe, and . . . it's an ongoing process. *(Andrew
Hope III, Sitka)*

One must realize that we are being invaded by the Western world.
We have to build some kind of a foundation that's solid, that will
not crumble beneath our children's feet. Some kind of a long-term
relationship with the American government, State of Alaska, to get
adjusted to the Western world, to have the power to balance between taxpayers and welfare, to get the education that our children
need. *(Ernie Tritt, Arctic Village)*

Alaska Natives are weary of the competition among governmental institutions at the village level. Authority is diffused.
Besides a tribal government, in the form of a traditional council

or an IRA council, there is often a state-chartered local government, as well as local and regional school boards and committees, regional fish and game advisory boards, health boards, and many information-gathering organizations associated with a wide variety of state and federal programs. All of them make heavy demands on the villages and on their leaders.

In addition, there are ANCSA's creations: the village and regional corporations. They, too, make heavy demands on the village leaders, demands that often place them in positions of conflict in which they must represent both the village and the corporation. There are also Native regional non-profit corporations, organized before and after ANCSA, which contract with state and federal agencies to administer a variety of social services.

> I've had titles that I mentioned earlier, being the president of the village corporation, the president of the IRA, the mayor, the manager for a tribal council, manager for Stebbins Native Corporation, and the list goes on . . . we've had meetings about—I think about six meetings a month—in different organizations. And I tell you, it becomes a headache after a while. Every time you see them, you change your hat. Because you're the mayor, and then you go to a corporation, you change your hat again. You're vice-president or a member, and it's, you know, it's very hard to deal with multi or several organizations that are trying to do the same thing. *(Ted Katcheak, Stebbins)*

The sovereignty movement has arisen from a positive sense of communal Native identity, and frustration with the present confusion of corporations, municipalities, and the plethora of state agencies that can be traced, directly or indirectly, to ANCSA has encouraged it. Nora de'Witt, city clerk at Saxman (a Native village of about three hundred residents near Ketchikan), and secretary-treasurer of the local IRA government, asked:

> Who is the tribe? The state recognizes the City of Saxman but does not recognize the tribe, and some of these federal agencies recognize the village corporation as if it were a tribe. A tribe has sov-

ereignty, inherent powers, and is a recognized government, and it should be the only entity recognized as such. But I strongly feel the village corporation should not be addressed in this fashion, because [it] only represents the shareholders and is basically profit making. They are not a government, nor do they possess sovereignty, and they do not have inherent powers.

One of the main goals of PL 638 [the Indian Self-Determination and Education Assistance Act] was to enhance the tribes in self-determination and self-government with inherent powers. In order to accomplish this goal the tribes must be recognized as such. And allowed to develop. But, when there are agencies who interpret the tribe as the IRA, and yet give this same status to the village corporations formed under ANCSA, this adds to the struggle of the tribes in Alaska. This places a tribe and village corporation in direct competition for funding sources. Then, to further complicate the issue, in some areas there is not only a tribe and a village corporation, but also a regional corporation. Who in this situation would receive the funding? In my opinion, the one responsible for all Indian members of the community would be the tribe. But again I stress that this places three Native groups in direct competition for funding. What are we to do? Not only are we still struggling with the federal and state governments, but now there is this inner struggle.

Joseph Lomack, an Akiachak elder, said:

One of the basic problems in the IRA or the traditional-council structure versus the municipal corporations under the state has been the power play that has been dividing a lot of the Native communities to a point in which the social infrastructure has been so diluted, to a point wherein no direction is seen, and to a point where the Western culture now imposes, with its rules and regulations, as to how a society as a unit is going to live.

Generally, the conflict is between tribal government and state-chartered local government, although in many villages the same persons serve both bodies. In Tununak, Mike Albert, president of the IRA council, said: "We have two governments, and one of them has to go." Weaver Ivanoff, president of the IRA council in Unalakleet, said: "ANCSA mandated city governments. This gave us two councils to govern one village. It can't work. One has to swallow up the other."

Spud Williams, president of the Tanana Chiefs Conference, argues:

> As current failings indicate, it is not practical to assume that a municipal structure can address the tribal interest. It is possible, however, for the tribal structure to address the municipal interest. This is primarily because the tribal spectrum of concern is both greater than and inclusive of the municipal spectrum of concern. It is, therefore, possible for small Native villages, which have organized a municipal entity, to dissolve the city in deference to the tribal structure. This will eliminate many of the cities which operate in a tribal fashion. While these villages operate inefficiently as cities, they are efficient in the tribal sense. This is not because Natives can't run efficient municipal governments, but rather because Native perceptions about government and its role is different than non-Native perceptions. It is important to have governmental structures reflect the perceptions of the people that they serve, and we believe that, in many cases, the dissolution of cities in favor of tribal institutions would advance that cause.

The people of Akiachak are forcing the issue there. In 1983, the city council unanimously voted to dissolve itself and send its charter back to the state, despite a warning that they were jeopardizing their access to state funds. At the same time, they tried to assign all the city's assets to the IRA government. In July 1984, representatives of three villages, Akiachak, Akiak, and Tuluksak, held a meeting in which they formed a regional tribal federation. One Yup'ik village has recently advised state troopers not to enter it without permission; another intends to restrict bear hunting for sport. Language reinforces their sense of solidarity: Yup'ik is taught in the schools and nearly everyone speaks it. These Yup'ik people have moved further and faster in the direction of sovereignty than the Native peoples of other regions, but I heard the same point of view expressed everywhere in village Alaska.

> Many villages are now beginning to think along the lines of dissolution of cities, thus allowing the IRA, or traditional council, to be

in a position to exercise their sovereign power. It would be very difficult to exercise sovereign power over only people. Therefore, the next logical step might be to dissolve the village corporation and allow them to exercise sovereign power over not only people but land. This would provide one organization power base in each village with sovereign authority over the people and, of course, the land. They would also be eligible for state and federal funding. *(Gary T. Longley, Sr., Council)*

Native sovereignty is also important to the State of Alaska. Tribal government is the conduit for the special programs available to Native Americans. The Supreme Court has stated that, if these programs are based on race, they might well be unconstitutional. In fact, they are based on a political relationship between the federal government and the Native peoples. If the federal government had no special obligation to provide social and health services to Alaska Natives, the State of Alaska, as a practical matter, would have to provide them. The state's opposition to Native sovereignty, if successful, would eliminate the special relationship between the tribal governments and the federal government, a result that could only damage the state by denying federal financial resources that every state in the Lower 48 that has a Native American population now receives. The state would then be obliged to fulfill obligations that more properly rest with the federal government.

If the principle of Native sovereignty is acknowledged to be legitimate, if tribal governments are acknowledged to be legitimate, why should Natives who participate in them not retain all of their rights as citizens of Alaska? No one has ever suggested that the citizens of Alaska who acknowledge the state's sovereignty should be disqualified from receiving federal funds. Why, then, should citizens of Alaska, who are also members of a tribe, not receive the services of the state?

Tribal government could also serve as a conduit for state-funded services even to non-Natives. There is some concern that, to avoid discrimination, all persons who receive services from an entity should be eligible for membership in it. Tribal governments can, and in Alaska they do, provide services to non-members without discrimination. In any event, conditions to ensure non-discrimination can be reasonably attached to any state grant, contract, or loan. It is unreasonable, however, to assume that a tribal government will discriminate against non-members, and unreasonable for the state to require tribes to dismantle traditional governments to ensure non-members a role in all local decisions as a condition for the receipt of funding from state programs. The state can always enforce compliance by cutting off aid. The threat of such action should be sufficient to prevent abuses.

The state has already taken steps along these lines in the case of Metlakatla. The tribal government of Metlakatla has long been excluded from Alaska's municipal assistance program because it is not chartered under state law as a municipality. In 1985, the Alaska legislature enacted a statute to permit Metlakatla to charter its own corporation under tribal law and to share state revenue as a municipality. Under this legislation, the tribal corporation must be excluded from any protection offered by the tribe's sovereign immunity so that the state can recover any funds improperly used. The corporation must be open to participation by all residents of the community, whether or not they are members of the tribe. Here is the first example in Alaska of a tribally chartered institution legally permitted to serve as a municipality for state political purposes. It seems that the state has taken the first step to accommodate tribal government.

Because tribes are governments in their own right, states may delegate some of their own functions to them. Florida, Idaho, Maine, Montana, New York, South Dakota, and Wisconsin have done so in varying degrees. In 1984, the Navajo Tribal Council and the governments of Arizona, New Mexico, and Utah signed a statement of policy that endorsed a government-to-government relationship. The legislature of North Dakota has recently authorized intergovernmental agreements with tribal governments. The Alaska legislature has recognized this inherent political status of village tribal governments by enacting legislation that entitles a "Native village council" in a community where there is no municipal government to an annual grant of $25,000. Several Alaska statutes authorize state loans to village councils in such a community.

How, in practice, would tribal government work in Alaska?

At Metlakatla, a tribal council exercises sovereignty over the tribal lands, and it decides who can be a member of the Native Community of Metlakatla. Membership is restricted to Native persons. Native families apply to the council for permits to use home sites; they may be sold, but only with the consent of the council (in effect, only improvements are sold). Non-Natives who marry Natives are entitled to live in the community, and they are given permits to work in the cannery during summer or to occupy positions in local government that require special skills. The community has the power to levy taxes on property and an income tax. Non-Natives cannot vote in tribal elections, but of course Natives and non-Natives alike have the right to vote in state and federal elections.

Some Americans react negatively to the very idea of Native governments, considering them to be an aberration in the American political system. But, as John Marshall said, the Native nations are not foreign; they have been a part of American political arrangements for more than two hundred years. Indeed, it is impossible to make the case for distinctive Native institutions of government and distinctive Native forms of land ownership unless it is based on firm intellectual foundations. We cannot begin with a recital of past injustices, repeat once more the usual statistics for Native social pathologies, and end with a plea for equal protection. Such an argument, persuasive enough in its own terms, cannot settle conflicts over land and self-government. Unless the Native peoples' case is based on sovereignty, its champions will find themselves disarmed when they come on to the real battleground.

Some persons fear that a recommendation to acknowledge Native sovereignty in Alaska may give rise to false hopes among Alaska Natives. To speak of false hopes with respect to the realization of Native sovereignty within American constitutional arrangements is like speaking of false hopes with respect to the realization of individual freedoms within the same constitutional arrangements. As Professor Ted Chamberlin has said, "For aboriginal peoples the world over, most certainly for Alaska Natives, sovereignty is fresh air and freedom to breathe."

It is foolish to assume that people do not mean what they say. It is tempting to dismiss as empty rhetoric what we do not understand or do not want to understand. When the Native peoples speak of sovereignty, they mean something. They know that, as peoples who have occupied their lands for tens of thousands of years, as peoples with a world view, customs, and institutions that persist to this day, they are entitled to a greater measure of control over their own lives, their own lands, and their own communities. As Sheldon Katchatag, president of the United Tribes of Alaska, said:

> We are not to be assimilated solely because that great government in Washington, D.C., says that is to be their policy. Even if the Congress decides to enact . . . that there will be no more IRA governments, there will still be tribal governments, because that is the will of the people.

It is apparent that many Alaska Natives hold high hopes for what can be achieved under tribal government. It is apparent that they believe tribal government will protect their interests better than ANCSA corporations or state-chartered local governments can. I believe they are right to think so. No one believes that tribal government can solve all the problems in the villages. Tribal government is, however, essential to the recommendations I intend to make regarding the future of Native lands and Native subsistence. But, beyond those objectives, it will be up to Native people to decide what use they will make of tribal government.

Seven

RECOMMENDATIONS

We are the only ones who can save ourselves. We keep looking to the outside world for someone to come and do it, and it is not going to happen. We are expecting someone out there to save us and, in fact, there is nothing in the outside world that is really that important. . . . I think our people ought to understand that it is possible to maintain their identity and their spirit and their language and their traditions and their history and their values and still function in the twenty-first century. We know what we need to know, how to make decisions, how to analyze situations, how to speak many languages and understand technology. *(Edgar Ningeulook, Shishmaref)*

Tununak and Fairbanks have very different Native communities. In one, the great majority is Native people who still live off the land; in the other, Natives are a minority within a large urban population. To the people of Tununak, subsistence and self-government are the paramount issues; to the Native community within Fairbanks, these concerns are less pronounced. Both of them, however, share a common concern to keep Native land in Native ownership.

The concepts articulated by John Marshall offer an answer to the dilemma ANCSA has presented to village Alaska: distinctive institutions of self-government and distinctive modes of land tenure. This is what distinguishes Native Americans in law from other minorities. The egalitarian measures used to address the just demands of ethnic minorities are inadequate for Native Americans.

The Distinctiveness of Native Americans

The United States takes pride in being a natural home for peoples of any religion or race, any language or culture. Immigrants in their millions have come to the United States. As individuals, as families, they chose America and its institutional arrangements. Native Americans are not a minority in the same sense. They did not choose America. They were here first, with their own societies, laws, and institutions, and they wish to remain distinct. But immigrant minorities have consciously worked to integrate themselves in the great melting pot of American society.

Black Americans were brought to the United States as slaves. But, separated by an ocean from their ancestral lands, they have no legal claim to a land base or jurisdiction of their own in America. Their goal, during the past century, has been equality of opportunity, equality as individuals. Their struggle, seen on television, is central to present-day urban life in America. Many Americans rallied to the Black civil-rights movement during the 1960s because they could see that Black Americans wanted the same rights as other Americans. Their struggle serves as an example for other minorities in the United States who demand equal access to political institutions and economic opportunities. It is vital to understand, however, that the goals of Black Americans are different in many ways from the goals of Native Americans.

The struggle of Native peoples takes place far from the consciousness of most Americans, on rural reservations glimpsed from the highway, or, in Alaska, in villages on the edge of the Arctic Ocean, where few White Americans have been—off camera, so to speak. There are no marches down the main streets. The desire of Native Americans to remain distinct political communities has frustrated those who have attempted to lead them along the road Black Americans have taken.

Many Americans believe that to claim rights for tribes or classes, groups or collectivities, runs against the American individualist tradition. They consider that the protection of individual rights is the most effective way to secure such interests. Legal and constitutional means to protect these rights for minorities in the United States are expressed in laws to prevent discrimination on the basis of race, nationality, or color, and in laws to protect the free exercise of religion. Although Native Americans from time to time claim the benefit of these laws, their central concerns do not fall within these categories.

Native rights rest on a fundamentally different footing from the claims of Black Americans and immigrant minorities. Their attempts to preserve, on their own terms and for their own purposes, a land-based culture and way of life mark Native

Americans off from other minorities. No other minority can assert a right to a land base and to distinct political institutions founded on the recognition of Native sovereignty.

President Reagan, in a policy statement issued in January 1983, reiterated the sovereignty of tribal governments. Yet, in Juneau and even in Washington, D.C., a tendency to deny the legitimacy of Native sovereignty in Alaska continues. How could the expression "sovereignty" be used in a carefully constructed policy statement related to Native Americans and not apply to those in Alaska? It is neither logically consistent nor morally defensible to deny to Alaska Natives the rights held by other Native Americans. Some persons say that Alaska Natives are unlike American Indians: their goals are different and they wish to integrate. That is not what Alaska Natives have been telling me. Their goals are fundamentally the same as those of American Indians as well as those of related peoples throughout the Canadian and Greenland Arctic and sub-Arctic and indigenous peoples the world over. In the preamble to the Indian Self-Determination and Education Assistance Act, 1975, Congress declared that "the Indian people will never surrender their desire to control their relationships both among themselves and with non-Indian governments, organizations, and persons." It seems unlikely that Alaska Natives have surrendered what Indians of the Lower 48 have fought to preserve.

Is America willing to acknowledge the persistence of Native culture and Native values in Alaska, the legitimacy of distinct modes of Native landholding and Native governance as essential expressions of Native culture and values? Does America's cultural pluralism extend to all of its indigenous peoples? These questions underlie the riddles of ANCSA, and they will not go away. The stand that Alaskans and other Americans adopt will be based on their own deepest convictions about their nation.

These issues are not partisan. Both the Republican and the Democratic parties, from Franklin Roosevelt to Ronald Reagan, have espoused the cause of Native Americans. Conservatives have an interest in conserving indigenous institutions that have worked for centuries. Liberals should understand that to undermine Native institutions is to undermine their cultural identity and, in that way, to erode Native individual identity.

Retribalization of Land

In general, the Native persons who testified at the hearings I held throughout Alaska want to sever Native lands from the ANCSA corporations; many of them want to retribalize their lands by transferring them to tribal governments. In this desire, they perceive an answer that is logical not only in their eyes, but also in the eyes of the law. If the corporations keep the land, it will not remain in Native hands. Alaska Natives require a form of landholding that reflects their own cultural imperatives and ensures that ancestral lands will remain in their possession, under their own governance. The road to the retribalization of Native land is plain, its implications clear; this way, there is a legal path, not a legal thicket.

All that I have written in preceding chapters reveals the chaos that will result if shares in the village corporations are to be sold. To accept that as if it were simply a case of exercising personal choice in an ordinary matter of private law is to use the vocabulary of corporate law to obscure the cultural consequences that would ensue in the villages. Native people may accept private-law instruments for disposing of units of wealth, but this willingness does not eradicate their continuing attachment to the land. It may be something that White culture expects of them; it doesn't nullify the deeper impulse of Native culture. If there is to be a right to sell shares, it must be only to sell shares in a village corporation that has divested itself of its ancestral lands by conveying them to a tribal government. Surprisingly, many urban Natives urged this idea: the theme struck by many was "Keep the land in Native ownership, but let me sell my shares." In this way, the land would stay in Native hands, even though shareholders would still have the right "to get out of the system."

Under Alaska state law, shareholders who object to the transfer of ANCSA land to a tribal government would have the right to be bought out at market value. Congress has the power under the Commerce Clause to authorize retribalization of ANCSA land without regard to the rights of dissenting shareholders under Alaska state law. In 1973, Congress restored the Menominees' tribal government and extinguished the right of dissenting shareholders to be bought out. It has already exercised this power in Alaska in the 1976 legislation authorizing mergers of ANCSA corporations without regard to dissenters' rights. It will have to exercise it again to enable the villages to retain their land.

It should be understood, however, that if village corporation land is transferred to tribal governments, the economic development of the land may in the future be harder to arrange than if the land were still under corporate ownership. This is, in a sense, the very object of the transfer. Nevertheless, there may be tracts of land that, in years to come, villages will want to improve or to develop. Obtaining capital or credit may not then be a straightforward business transaction, as it is for a corporation. A waiver of sovereign immunity with respect to the land to be developed might be required. This is not to say that tribal governments cannot develop land. Many in the Lower 48 do. Others operate businesses—indeed, the tribal government at Metlakatla operates a cannery.

Self-Government

A corporation cannot take from the rich and give to the poor without facing a shareholders' suit; but a tribal government can implement measures designed to achieve social justice. A corporation can claim no immunity to state laws—it is a creature of state laws—but a tribal government can assert immunity from them. A profit-making corporation is comprised of stockholders who own shares; but a tribal government is comprised of members identified by who they are, not what they own. A corporation's existence depends upon statements of its profit and loss, but a tribe's existence is endlessly renewed with each generation. All of these are reasons why Alaska Natives have told me they want tribal governments.

But even if corporations are rejected as the primary means for holding Native lands, why should tribal governments be preferred to state-chartered local governments as the expression of Native political interests? The issue of public government, as against Native government, arose at virtually all the hearings.

At Barrow, many persons pointed out the advantages that a home-rule borough had brought to the Inupiat Eskimos who live there. These advantages derive from two main reasons: the Inupiat form the majority in the North Slope Borough and they have a tax base, revenue from the production of oil at Prudhoe Bay.

The North Slope Borough may be regarded as the first beach-head of Eskimo home rule in the Arctic. There have been others since then. In 1975, the Inuit (Eskimos) of northern Quebec established a regional government, Kativik, where they constitute ninety percent of the population. In 1978, the Inuit of Greenland, who constitute eighty percent of the population, established a home-rule government.

The Eskimos of the North Slope Borough, northern Quebec, and Greenland chose public government as a means of achieving Eskimo home rule because they constitute a majority of the population. They will probably continue to do so because they live in some of the world's least habitable regions. Otherwise, I believe, they would have chosen a form of Native government. Indeed, in northern Quebec, the Cree, who settled their claim at the same time as the Inuit, opted for a tribal form of government because they are a minority in their region.

In the North Slope Borough, the question of an appropriate vehicle for holding ANCSA land is important: after the land becomes taxable during the 1990s, the borough (whether or not its government eventually falls into non-Native hands) may be obliged to levy a property tax on all taxable real estate within its boundaries on a non-discriminatory basis. Together, the regional corporation and the village corporations on the North Slope own approximately 5.5 million acres. Ronald Brower, vice-president in charge of land for the village corporation in Barrow, referring to the possibility that ANCSA lands might have to be taxed by the borough, said: "After 1991, you might as well turn over all [Native] lands to the borough."

At this point in Alaska, Native sovereignty has clear advantages over public government, even where Natives constitute a majority. Whatever else may be said about public governments, they do not own the Native land. If tribal governments on the North Slope owned ANCSA village land, the land would be immune from taxation by the North Slope Borough. In some cases, there is no reason why tribal and public governments should not exist side by side, just as, in Wisconsin, the Menominee retained their state-chartered county government even after their tribal government was restored.

Notwithstanding these uses of state institutions, the Native peoples of Alaska clearly want their own tribal governments. The political character of these governments is an aspect of the peoples' identity, just as languages and cultures are. Their own political institutions are essential to their tribal character, without which they are no more than a collection of some seventy thousand individuals of various races and languages, a minority like any other, with no claim to land nor to distinct institutional arrangements. But, in fact, they are tribes. If they were not tribes, if they were nothing more than Natives scattered around Alaska, if their political organization did not define who they are, then their position really would be indistinguishable from that of any immigrant minority. As such, they are entitled to claim the right—and assume the burdens—of governing themselves. As Osage-Otoe attorney Browning Pipestem told the commission:

> Being a government is a problem. It's not fun being a government. It's a serious undertaking. . . . If you are [a tribal government], then it seems to me that you need to exercise your authority. If you are not, then you need to forget about it. . . . The . . . growth of tribal government has come . . . as the Indian people have better understood the nature of the authority that they have exercised.

Alaska Natives must be ready to assume responsibility as sovereign peoples, and Congress must fully acknowledge that, in Alaska as in the Lower 48, Native governments are legitimate political institutions, and that they have a right to retain ancestral lands in perpetuity. The blend of institutional arrangements is not likely to be the same in Alaska as it is for Indians in the Lower 48. Such an affirmation would nevertheless be wholly consistent with the principles of federalism that undergird the American political system.

Subsistence: Native Jurisdiction over Fish and Wildlife

Native governments are also essential if Native peoples are to defend subsistence. The State of Alaska is unable to defend Native subsistence, municipalities will not do it, and the corporations cannot do it.

Native peoples already have the exclusive right to take fish and wildlife resources on Native-owned lands and water, subject to state jurisdiction. This means that although they are the only ones who can fish, hunt, trap, and gather on the ten percent of Alaska that they own, the state tells them when, what, and how much they can harvest. They want the right to manage these resources themselves. I think they should have exclusive jurisdiction over fish and wildlife on ANCSA lands. There, they should manage the resources themselves.

Tribal members, by virtue of tribal membership, would have the exclusive right to fish and wildlife on Native lands and waters. The tribal government could, of course, extend these rights to urban Natives and others. Since Native governments would own these lands, exclusive rights and jurisdiction seem altogether appropriate, but these lands comprise only ten percent of the state and are inadequate for Native subsistence. Native people must have guaranteed access to their other fishing, hunting, trapping, and gathering areas on state and federal lands. Also, in partnership with state and federal authorities, they should share jurisdiction over fish and wildlife in those areas. There are distinct advantages for the state in such an arrangement. As Spud Williams, president of Tanana Chiefs, said:

> The state needs us as much as we need them to manage fish and game resources. They've got to be willing to recognize tribal governments for effective management in rural Alaska. They cannot police this country. The only police force out there that can do it are the people, and we are probably more strict than the state in watching our food because . . . it's not fish and game, it's food. We are not going to let somebody destroy our table, so we have to maintain those authorities and those functions. The state is too large for the state to do it. The state can't even take care of

Anchorage and Fairbanks and Juneau and the major communities,
let alone take care of rural Alaska. They don't have the resources
to do it, they don't have the manpower. They can't do it. They need
the cooperation of the people to do it. And they have to cooperate
with us, and then we will cooperate with them—it's that simple.
It's going to take a partnership or they are going to destroy our
state.

Simply put, the members of Alaska Native tribes ought to
have exclusive hunting and fishing rights and jurisdiction over
Native lands and waters, and shared rights and jurisdiction over
state and federal lands and waters. There are precedents that
have been successful elsewhere.

Treaty fishing rights in the state of Washington are among the
notable examples. In *Passenger Fishing Vessel Owners Association
v. Washington,* the U.S. Supreme Court had to consider several
treaties made in 1855 that entitle members of the signatory
tribes to fish off their reservations at their "usual and accus-
tomed grounds and stations in common with the citizens of the
territory." The court held that this language meant the signatory
tribes were entitled to the opportunity to take up to fifty percent
of the harvestable catch (after spawning escapement) within
waters covered by the treaties, nearly all the salmon-fishing
waters in Washington. To exercise these rights, tribal fishermen
need not buy state fishing licenses, and they are also entitled to
fish from their traditional fishing stations, whether located on
private or publicly owned lands.

Tribal fishing rights have also been applied to species that,
unlike salmon, can be caught only in the ocean. In 1984, the
Makah Indians of western Washington obtained federal recognition of tribal rights to harvest fish at "their usual and accus-
tomed" fishing grounds off the Washington coast under this
same series of treaties. The courts have also upheld the jurisdiction of the western Washington tribes to regulate the fishing
rights of their own members on and off the reservation, free
from state control, as long as the tribes have their own courts,
laws, and law-enforcement systems.

The affirmation of these treaty rights has revitalized the Native economies and societies in western Washington. Moreover,

the twenty-two tribes have established research and enhancement programs that have benefited all users of the fishery. The tribes participate with state and federal authorities in a management plan that applies to all waters affected by the treaties. Similar management regimes for both hunting and fishing are possible and desirable in Alaska and have been recently implemented in Canadian settlements with Native peoples of the Arctic and sub-Arctic.

Under the James Bay Agreement of 1975, the Cree and Inuit of northern Quebec received land in fee simple (the Inuit received two million acres, the Cree about one million acres), and the exclusive right to hunt, fish, and trap on an additional thirty-eight million acres. Because there are only about ten thousand Cree and Inuit, these rights are significant. Even beyond these lands, the Natives have the exclusive right to hunt, fish, and trap certain species of fish and wildlife. The Inuit also exercise jurisdiction over these activities according to their own customs and laws. Harvest levels, quotas, and wildlife management are largely their responsibility.

Under the Western Arctic Claim of 1984, the Inuvialuit have exclusive rights to wildlife on their own lands and preferential rights to all wildlife in the whole of the western Arctic region. They also have exclusive rights to bear and musk-ox in the region. All of these rights are subject to laws of general application for safety and conservation. The point is that, in these recent settlements, the right of Native people to take wildlife is not confined to the lands to which they received title under the settlement, but in order to protect their way of life—their culture—it includes areas within the public domain that they have always used.

Native jurisdiction over subsistence activities carries with it a responsibility for their management. Native government can undertake the direct management of fish and wildlife resources, providing local control over their resources by the people who have the greatest interest in their preservation. Through regulations or practices that reflect local considerations, Native governments can effectively improve the protection of wildlife habitat and reduce the cost of wildlife management in remote areas of Alaska. It will, as Oscar Kawagley said at the hearing in

Bethel, "take the natural talents our people have and put them to work in the sciences."

I think the people are certainly excellent land managers. They can certainly take care of the game, the land, and they have proved that by doing it over the last—who knows how long?—forever, I suppose, and . . . our people's knowledge isn't really being utilized to its fullest. *(Wayne Attla, Hughes)*

I also feel that Fish and Game shouldn't put regulations for the people. I feel that our people could do a better job than some college graduate that comes here to put regulations on us. I also feel that all the regulations could be made by the Native people that live on the land, and could be much better off than that which is written from Washington, D.C., or Juneau. Those laws we don't get along with. I am sure if we were to write our own laws, we would be much more happier. *(Louis Commack, Ambler)*

Because most Native lands are bounded by immense tracts of federal and state land, cooperative planning to manage and protect the interests of all parties will be necessary and desirable. For example, the values and standards of national parks could be maintained on Native lands, and the values and standards of Native subsistence could, at the same time, be maintained on park lands. To realize this goal, tribal governments should be able to contract with state and federal agencies to conduct scientific studies and management activities that are required for migratory species.

Under the Indian Reorganization Act, tribes have the authority to negotiate agreements with the state and federal governments. Under the Lacey Act, which applies to Alaska, federal fish and wildlife enforcement agencies are authorized to contract with tribes and their members to use their services and their facilities to jointly enforce federal laws prohibiting the interstate transport of fish and wildlife taken in violation of tribal law. There is no reason why the state cannot contract with tribal governments to regulate fish and wildlife; it is simply a matter of passing a statute to authorize state agencies to do so. Many states with Native populations already have such laws.

We have seen how Congress has, in the past, restored tribal rights after periods of experimentation with other regimes. In ANCSA, aboriginal rights to hunt and fish were extinguished. In ANILCA, the cultural entitlement of Native people in Alaska to fish and wildlife resources was recognized and partially restored. Now the time has come to fully implement that finding by restoring tribal rights to fish and wildlife resources.

Recommendations

In making recommendations, there is a danger of entanglement in the web of issues that ANCSA presents: shares, dissenters' rights, the land bank, children born after 1971—the list could go on—but the main concerns of Alaska Natives, and therefore of this book, are land, self-government, and subsistence. These concerns are linked: taken together, they are the means by which the Native people seek to regain control over their land, their communities, and their lives. Dealing with them offers at the same time an opportunity to make recommendations regarding the future of the Native corporations.

I am not recommending the transfer of any additional lands from the public domain to Native ownership. What concerns me here is the fate of the forty-four million acres to be conveyed to Native ownership by ANCSA. It is likely that the Native peoples of Haines, Seward, Wrangell, Petersburg, and Ketchikan, all of whom were excluded from ANCSA and received no lands, will submit claims that may have to be addressed. The special-purpose lands allocated under ANCSA may be sufficient to provide lands for these communities.

I am recommending that Congress reexamine some issues related to compensation. The complexity of the legislation resulted in the dissipation of a great deal of the financial compensation in legal action; delays in conveying land caused losses in earnings; and high inflation during the payout phase reduced the total monetary settlement by nearly a third. Congress could establish a fund to pay the debts of Native corporations whose lands are in jeopardy. The Treasury could be reimbursed from future revenues, including revenues under Section 7(j) of

ANCSA. Even so, money is not the solution. The persons who spoke at the hearings were chiefly concerned about the land, self-government, and subsistence, and it is right, I think, to concentrate on these subjects.

Recommendations: Land

Since the land is now a corporate asset, the scope of possible recommendations is limited. It is not possible simply to urge that a law should be passed transferring the land from Native corporations to tribal governments. The land is, under the law, private property belonging to the corporations. My recommendations are, therefore, addressed to the Native shareholders in the corporations. Given congressional action, it will be possible for the Native people to unscramble the omelet.

I recommend that the shareholders of village corporations who are concerned that their land may be lost should transfer their land to tribal governments to keep the land in Native ownership. The matter is one of urgency in the villages, and it should be done at once. The tribal government would hold this land in fee simple, although some tribes may wish to place their land in trust with the federal government. In either case, the tribal government would be able to claim sovereign immunity with respect to the land. Congress should pass legislation to facilitate the transfer of land by the village corporations to tribal governments without regard for dissenters' rights. Where village corporations have merged, the lands formerly held by each village corporation should be transferred by the merged corporation to the appropriate tribal governments.

Tribal governments would exercise all of the functions of the corporations with respect to any further village-land selections and conveyances. Land should be turned over to tribal governments on condition that they admit to membership all of the original shareholders in the village corporation. Tribal governments have the power to determine their own membership, and Natives born after 1971 should be members of a tribe. This arrangement accommodates the children born after 1971; they should be included in the tribe by virtue of their being born into it.

Congress should enact legislation to clarify the village tribal governments' right to exercise a veto power over all subsurface development on village-owned ANCSA lands. Village corporations presently have such a right under Section 14(f) of ANCSA, but it is not clear that this right extends to all village corporation lands.

I recommend that the lands required by Section 14(c)(3) of ANCSA to be conveyed to state-chartered local governments or to the state in trust should be transferred to the tribal government. Any land already conveyed for this purpose should be reconveyed by the local government or the state to a tribal government. Unoccupied federal townsite lands in unincorporated communities or in communities that dissolve their municipalities should also be conveyed to the tribal governments. Unless those entitled were to waive their entitlements to fee land, the tribal government would be required to make the other conveyances under ANCSA Section 14(c) to protect the interests of residents and local businesses. The airport reconveyances required under Section 14(c)(4) should go to the tribal governments.

Recommendations: Village Corporations

Because my recommendations relate only to the land, they would leave the village corporations and the merged corporations with all their other business assets. If a village corporation has a thriving business or investments, nothing I have said would impair the corporation's right to continue to carry on its business, to make a profit, and to pay dividends to shareholders. In most cases, however, it seems likely that, without their land, the village corporations will be dissolved.

If a village corporation is already engaged in profitable activities based on land development, the land, after it is transferred to the tribal government, can be leased back to the corporation for business purposes. The tribal government would also have the option of chartering a tribal corporation to take over the operations of the village corporation.

If the village dissolves its corporation and transfers all of its assets to the tribal government, the tribal government should receive revenues otherwise due the village corporation under ANCSA Section 7(j).

Recommendations: Regional Corporations

I have concerned myself principally with the future of the villages, a concern that entails specific recommendations regarding the land that belongs to the village corporations. The regional corporations own the subsurface of the village lands and sixteen million acres of other land, much of which is checkerboarded with village lands. The regional corporations together have the right to select approximately one million acres of special-purpose lands, but they are of less importance to the villages. It is the village subsurface lands held by the regional corporations and the sixteen million acres adjacent to the village lands that are of concern to Native subsistence interests. If the regional corporation loses its lands, Native subsistence users would no longer have access to them; moreover, the new owner could use the lands in ways destructive to village interests.

Regional corporations should consider transferring the subsurface of village lands to the respective village tribal governments. If it were deemed advisable to keep the subsurface in some type of regional organization to continue the interlocking arrangement between regions and villages that Congress had in mind, an alternative would be to transfer the subsurface to a regional tribal government. If such an institution did not already exist, then the affected region would have to establish one, and this might require congressional action.

Regional corporations should also consider at least three options with respect to the sixteen million acres of wholly owned regional-corporation lands adjacent to the villages. First, they should consider transferring these lands to the villages to ensure unified village control of the greatest possible acreage. Second, the regional corporations should consider transferring these lands to regional tribal governments, perhaps in conjunction with the transfer of village corporation lands to village tribal governments, if it seemed important to maintain both village and regional land-owning institutions. Finally, the regional corporations should consider assigning subsistence easements to village or regional tribal governments. Regional corporations would then continue to own the lands, but use of the lands would be restricted to subsistence purposes. New owners of regional lands would have to honor the easement. Such easements would be similar to conservation easements, now familiar in the Lower 48, but might require amendments to state and federal law to ensure that regional corporations granting the easements would receive the same tax advantages afforded grantors of conservation easements.

None of these options appears to be exclusive of each other; they could be used singly or in combination, depending on the wishes of regional and village corporation shareholders. It should also be noted that these options could be implemented in a region where the village and regional corporations are merged. In such a region, all the shareholders participate in only one corporation, which owns all the interests in all the lands, so it would be easier then to decide which lands should be transferred to village ownership and which lands, if any, should be retained in regional control.

The establishment of regional tribal organizations, recognized as such under federal law, would also provide the regional corporations with the option of assigning non-real estate assets with a view to securing the advantages of tribal immunity. The regional tribalization of lands should also be considered from the standpoint of the at-large shareholders for whom the loss of these lands may be especially significant.

Recommendations: Self-Government

Tribal governments established in all of Alaska's Native villages should assert their Native sovereignty.

Pending and future applications by villages in Alaska for tribal constitutions and charters under the Indian Reorganization Act should be granted. The state should recognize tribal governments as appropriate local governments for all purposes under state law. These measures, important for Native self-rule, may entail the dissolution of some, but not all, of the state-chartered local governments in Native villages.

I do not recommend the general establishment of Native reservations in Alaska. Instead, tribal governments would hold the land in fee simple. But if there are villages that want their land taken in federal trust, this should be done.

I urge that all land subject to the jurisdiction of Native governments should be described as Indian Country or, as the case may be, Eskimo Country or Aleut Country. This phrase would accurately describe the situation, and it would release everyone from a vocabulary that now confines the discussion of alternatives.

Recommendations: Subsistence

I recommend that tribal governments should have exclusive jurisdiction over fish and wildlife on Native lands, whether owned by Native corporations or by tribal governments. On federal and state lands (ninety percent of Alaska's land area), Native governments in partnership with state and federal governments should exercise jurisdiction on all hunting, trapping, and gathering lands used by tribal members. On all Native lands, the Native peoples would have the exclusive right, as tribal members, to subsistence, subject to exclusive tribal jurisdiction.

Exclusive Native rights, although appropriate for Native-owned lands and waters, are not appropriate for state and federal lands and waters in Alaska, because Native peoples do not own these areas and their claims to them have been extinguished. A different regime is required here, one that would fully protect the Native peoples' interests. Rights of access on state and federal lands and waters and a share of the resources fully sufficient for Native subsistence must be guaranteed. Shared jurisdiction with the state and federal governments should be exercised so that Native hunting and fishing rights are not regulated except for conservation purposes. Native authorities should impose and enforce regulations before federal or state authorities intervene. The James Bay and Northern Quebec

Agreement is perhaps the best model. The federal Marine Mammal Protection Act is an American example of a legal regime which intervenes in Native subsistence only when necessary.

The health and abundance of fish and wildlife depend on the quality of the environment throughout their range. Many species will migrate beyond Native-owned lands or lands used for Native subsistence within the state and federal domain. To ensure a continuing supply of subsistence resources for Alaska Natives, Congress must clearly establish a policy of protection for migratory species and provide for Native participation in the overseeing of that protection.

Eight /

THE FOURTH WORLD

This is what we have to do; we have got to look beyond the horizon because, when you look into the horizon, you think that is the end—but it is not. You walk to that horizon again, and there is another horizon. You can go all the way around the world in this manner. If we can look at it at that aspect, we will be better off. Otherwise, we will get too caught up in one simple thing, or one matter, or one problem. We have got to look at it from all angles. *(Robert Mulluk, Kotzebue)*

I would like to say that we have a long ways to go yet, and we cannot only look at small things—but world events, too. *(Frank Wright, Kotzebue)*

No one doubts that nations have rights, and there is general support today for the recognition of the rights of even the smallest nations. Like actors on an international stage, the nations of the world seem to assume personalities in the exercise of their rights. National constitutions affirm individual rights, and every thoughtful person would wish to see a universal recognition of individual rights in the constitutions of all nations. The rights of indigenous peoples fall somewhere between the rights of nations and individual rights, but they are intimately linked with both of them.

Old Questions

The history of Europe and the New World is more than the history of European nation-states, their conflicts, and their subjugation of the Americas, or of individuals like Columbus. It is the history of an encounter between the peoples of the Old World and the indigenous peoples of the New World. The expansion of the European powers, first Spain and Portugal, later France and England, into the New World raised the central question: By what right did Europeans take the land and subjugate the peoples of the New World? By what right did the Russians, and after them the Americans, lay claim to the lands of the Eskimos, Indians, and Aleuts of Alaska? Whether expanding westward or eastward, whether in the name of Christianity, civilization, or trade, the Europeans believed they had the right to dispossess peoples of other cultures.

To understand the issue of Native rights in North America today, we must go back to Bartolomé de Las Casas's "second discovery of America." In 1502, he sailed to America and there became one of the first to examine the relationship between Europeans and the indigenous peoples of the New World. The issues he raised, the rights of indigenous peoples, the destiny of Western man, the meaning of progress, still trouble us today.

Nearly five hundred years ago, Las Casas called upon the Spanish to consider by what right one race could impose its own laws and institutions on another race. We are struggling still with the implications of that question, though it does not arise in precisely the same terms as it did at the threshold of European occupation of the Native domain. We are still asking ourselves: What measures can be used to establish a fair and equitable relationship between dominant societies cast in the European mold and Native peoples?

Ever since the first Spanish conquests—since the time of Cortés and Pizarro—Europeans and their descendants have sought wealth on the frontiers of the New World to enrich the metropolis. Ever since, men have wished for another Montezuma's treasure, another Atahualpa to be ransomed. The search goes on today in Alaska for oil, gas, and minerals.

> Profit, as a motive for a nation geared to it, is a very powerful force that is quite boundless in its search for itself. It has built and destroyed nations and, in its path, it has left destruction and much sorrow for the people that live on the land, both the original inhabitants and those that chose to live there. What is happening now is following the path of those examples. *(Pete Schaeffer, Kotzebue)*

The governmental institutions that the Europeans established have reflected, and they still reflect, these values. We of the industrialized nations regard the city as a mirror of progress. This metropolitan model of economic development represents our own experience and, because of its demonstrated success, we believe that nations of the Third World should aspire to its achievements. And, of course, the model is one to which Native peoples who live within our own countries ought to aspire.

The industrial system that has created the great cities is not only a creator of wealth but also a shatterer of traditional societies and a powerful instrument of control in the new social systems to which it gives rise. It promises affluence, and it offers freedom from the constraints that nature and tradition have always imposed on humankind.

Today, the industrial system has spread all over the globe. Industrial man, the agent of change, armed with new technology and immense political and administrative power, is prepared to transform the social and natural landscape of the world to conform to the special demands of a particular kind of society and economy. Industrial man, equally the creature of the East and the West, is now at work to reshape the Third World. The governments of many Third World nations now share the commitment to endless growth, even though, for indisputable reasons, there may be no real prospect of achieving it.

Ideas born of the Industrial Revolution—those of Adam Smith and the *Communist Manifesto*—have led to the triumph of liberal capitalism, on the one hand, and to the challenge of Marxism, on the other. In the West, our traditions of democracy and due process, our belief in the rule of law, and our willingness to allow the market to make many important economic choices for us distinguish the industrialized democracies from the Soviet Union and its empire. Nevertheless, Western capitalism and Soviet communism are two forms of materialism, and they are competing for the allegiance of peoples throughout the world. Both seek to bring all citizens into the industrial economy.

With the advance of industry toward the last frontiers at a time when the indigenous peoples' ideas of self-determination are emerging in contemporary forms, the question of the relationship between dominant societies cast in the European mold and indigenous peoples confronts us again. Subsistence economies still exist in many parts of the world today, not yet altogether supplanted by the industrial system. Because we have a particular idea of progress, we have neglected to consider seriously the possibility of restructuring our own relations with traditional societies to ensure that their subsistence economies may not only be preserved but enabled to thrive.

Most Native peoples have no wish to assimilate. They have refused to be proletarianized. Their fierce desire to retain their own culture can only intensify as industry, technology, and communications forge a more deeply pervasive mass culture, excluding diversity of every kind. Native peoples the world over fear that, without political autonomy and their own land-based economy, they must be overwhelmed, facing a future that would have no place for the values they have always cherished. Native peoples everywhere insist that their own culture is still the vital force in their lives; the one fixed point in a changing world is their identity as Natives.

We humans are social animals. We define ourselves by knowing our own people, our language, our customs, our traditions. Culture is the comprehensive summary of standards, values, patterns of behavior, common attitudes, ways of life. Culture must have a material basis. This gives land claims a compelling urgency among the world's indigenous peoples. In September 1984, Pope John Paul II addressed Canada's Native peoples, a message that carried to indigenous peoples everywhere:

> You are entitled to a just and equitable measure of self-determination, with a just and equitable degree of self-governing. For you a land base with adequate resources is also necessary for developing a viable economy.

The Fourth World

With the independence of so many Third World nations, the condition and the claims of indigenous peoples who are locked into nations they can never hope to rule must now be considered. They constitute a Fourth World, and it extends from Alaska to Tierra del Fuego; it encompasses the Ainu of Japan, the Aborigine of Australia, the Maori of New Zealand, the Sami of Scandinavia, and the tribal peoples of the Soviet Union, China, India, and Southeast Asia.

Attempts by the indigenous peoples of the Fourth World to achieve self-determination face greater odds than most nations of the Third World have had to meet. Indigenous peoples of the Fourth World are usually minority populations within their own nations. Once the only inhabitants of their homelands, they have been overwhelmed by settler populations. They have survived long campaigns to persuade them to assimilate and persistent demands to subscribe to mass values. Often, especially in Latin America, governments have found it convenient to claim that an indigenous population within its boundaries has been completely absorbed.

Nations that have acknowledged individual rights have often opposed the recognition of indigenous peoples' rights because they imply territorial rights and a sovereignty in competition with that of the nation. Governments have often opposed the communal holding of land and criticized tribal institutions as neither democratic nor modern.

Some nations oppose recognition of indigenous rights ostensibly out of concern over the possibility of secession and a need for greater industrial development. Indigenous peoples do not usually struggle to separate from the nation-state nor to achieve independence within national boundaries; they want mainly to retain control over their own lives and their own land. Fourth World claims are claims to limited sovereignty, but they have not achieved the same recognition as Third World claims to full sovereignty.

Native claims and the idea of Native governments are not, as some believe, based on any kind of apartheid. In South Africa, Blacks are confined to so-called homelands without any right to citizenship in South Africa and without any right to live or work or to own property there. Blacks who live and work in South Africa do so on sufferance. The Native peoples of Alaska want their own lands and their own forms of government, and they also want access to the social, economic, and political institutions of the dominant society. Only if they are denied access to them could any suggestion of apartheid be made.

The struggles of indigenous peoples do not fit into convenient ideological or political categories. In the Soviet Union, as far back as the 1920s, the regime decided that the tribal councils of the indigenous peoples of Siberia were inimical to the Communist Party's goals of industrialization and assimilation. Native hunting and fishing rights were curtailed. National Areas were established, and the indigenous peoples brought within them. In these National Areas, which serve as regional governments executing central policy, non-Natives predominate. For instance, the Chukchis and the Eskimos, with a combined population of 12,000 in the Chukotsk National Area, are outnumbered by 70,000 Russians who control the Communist Party apparatus and the government of the area. In Nicaragua, the Miskito Indians are trying to establish a regional sovereignty within the nation. The Sandinista regime has described them as an ethnic minority, but the Miskitos insist they are an indigenous people. They will continue to assert their claim under the Sandinistas or any other regime.

In its own way, the reemergence of the Fourth World is as great a challenge to the West today as the reemergence of the Third World was during the period of decolonization, when so many Third World nations achieved independence. The relationship the indigenous peoples of the Fourth World seek, once achieved, cannot be carried on at arm's length; they must live side by side with and interact within the dominant society. Where indigenous people live in non-contiguous territory, as in Greenland or Papua New Guinea, and in some of the islands of Micronesia, the United Nations has helped them to achieve decolonization. Enclaves of indigenous peoples who live within a nation's boundaries cannot fit neatly into a standard pattern for decolonization. In the past, from the point of view of the international community, indigenous peoples were seen as requiring legal protection from economic exploitation, racial discrimination, and the denial of human rights. Today, with the support of international law, they are asserting rights to land and to their own institutions.

No sound theory of international law can justify the occupation of lands still inhabited by their aboriginal peoples. John Marshall was skeptical of the use of the rule of discovery to justify taking Indian land and limiting their sovereignty. Scholars have rejected the rule of discovery as a principle of international law. An alternative theory has described the lands of indigenous tribes as *terra nullius,* the land of no one. The

Australian courts have regarded their nation as having been unpeopled before 1788 or, if peopled, to have lacked any coherent system of law under which the land could belong to anyone. They treat the Australian Aborigines as if they had not existed or, if they had existed, as completely unorganized—notwithstanding the Aborigines' defense of their land against invaders.

In 1975, the International Court of Justice rejected the idea of *terra nullius* in the *Western Sahara* case. The question before the Court was whether or not, at the time of Spanish colonization in 1884, the Moroccan Western Sahara was a territory that belonged to no one, a *terra nullius.* The court held that it was not: nomadic peoples lived there who were socially and politically organized into tribes with chiefs competent to represent them. The court concluded that neither Mauretania nor Morocco had acquired any rights by any acceptable means from the original inhabitants.

The concept of self-determination is supplanting the discredited concepts of discovery and *terra nullius* in modern international law. President Woodrow Wilson espoused the idea of self-determination of peoples in the peace treaties that followed World War I and for the League of Nations. The Charter of the United Nations, to which the United States is a party, and which has the force of a treaty, affirms the idea of self-determination of peoples. In 1966, the General Assembly of the United Nations approved the International Covenant on Civil and Political Rights and the International Covenant on Cultural Rights, neither of which has yet been ratified by the United States. Both covenants assert the right of peoples to self-determination. The principle is reaffirmed in Article VIII of the Helsinki Accords of 1975, which are binding on the United States. It is the principle on which decolonization of the nations of the Third World has proceeded. The Helsinki Accords are administered by the Commission on Security and Cooperation in Europe, of which the United States is one of thirty-five member states. In testimony before the Commission in 1979 on U.S. compliance with the human rights provisions of the Helsinki Accords, Forrest Gerard, Assistant Secretary of the Interior for Indian Affairs, acknowledged the application of Article VIII to the self-determination of Native Americans.

In 1971, the United Nations authorized a special study on discrimination against indigenous populations. This action represents the United Nations' clear decision to separate questions related to indigenous peoples from the problems of racial discrimination. The claims of indigenous peoples can now be addressed as separate and distinct concerns at this international level. Since 1982, a United Nations Working Group on Indigenous Populations has met once a year in Geneva to formulate standards for the treatment of indigenous populations. In April 1985, Madame Erica Daes, chairperson of this working group, speaking in Quebec City, said that, in her opinion, the principle of the self-determination of peoples applied also to indigenous populations, although it did not include the right of secession.

Article 27 of the United Nations' International Covenant on Civil and Political Rights also reaches the special situation of Native or indigenous peoples; specifically, it upholds the right of a minority "to enjoy their own culture."

> In those states in which ethnic, religious or linguistic minorities exist, persons belonging to such minorities shall not be denied the right, in community with the other members of their group, to enjoy their own culture, to profess and practice their own religion, or to use their own language.

In my opinion, Article 27 applies to indigenous cultures that are closely linked to their land and its resources. If an indigenous people's loss of their land inevitably leads to the extinguishment of their distinct culture, the nation that took their land has violated Article 27 of this covenant. Nations have an obligation to protect traditional forms of economic activity on which the cultural integrity of indigenous peoples depend. It is arguable that the principles reflected in Article 27 have entered the body of customary international law and are binding even on those nations that have not yet signed the Covenant. Whether or not they have, the article is ample demonstration that indigenous peoples, in their search for self-determination, occupy the moral high ground.

Many nations are fleshing out commitments to protect Native lands and to increase Native autonomy. The new Canadian

constitution, adopted in 1982, has entrenched the existing aboriginal and treaty rights of Canada's indigenous peoples, and
a series of First Ministers' Conferences (meetings of the Prime
Minister with the provincial premiers), which Native leaders
have attended, have focused on Native self-government. During
the short life of the Alaska Native Review Commission, events
of this kind have followed one after another: in 1984, the report
of the Sami Rights Committee in Norway, and in February
1985, the Australian government's statement of policy on aboriginal land rights. There are stirrings in places where these
issues were thought to be dormant. A federal report in 1983
denying Native Hawaiian land rights, far from quelling the
land-claims movement, has fueled it. A government commission
is now at work in northern Japan to consider the rights of the
Ainu. The coincidence of these several developments is striking;
they will serve as a foundation for the continued development
of international law on indigenous peoples.

Current Questions

The clock cannot be turned back nor can the rule of discovery
be vitiated on any retroactive basis: the reality of effective occupation stands in the way. Nevertheless, some measure of self-
rule could be accorded to Native peoples within the constitutional framework of any Western nation. The Native peoples are
making many proposals, and some of them reach far. They
encompass renewable and non-renewable resources, education,
health, social services, and public order and they extend to the
shape and structure of political institutions. Proposals of this
kind are no threat to established institutions. We should regard
them as opportunities to affirm our commitment to the human
rights of indigenous peoples.

Many persons are inclined to dismiss Native claims of every
kind as so many attempts to secure present advantages by the
revival of ancient wrongs. Why should anyone today feel guilty
because of events that occurred long ago? Arguments of this
kind are beside the point. The question is not one of guilt,
present or past. The question is one of continuing injustice, and

the distinctive feature of the injustices, past and present, done to indigenous peoples is the fact that these injustices were committed against peoples. These peoples are still with us, and the nations that committed these injustices are still with us in one form or another. The injustices continue, and they are within the power of remedy.

The Europeans came to America, and on grounds that would be unacceptable today, they occupied lands that belonged to the Native peoples. The Russians did the same thing in Siberia and Alaska. If we wish to live in a world based on the rule of law, we must acknowledge that the claims of the Native peoples of the New World are not ancient, half-forgotten, and specious. They are, in fact, current and contemporary. Arguments for the rule of law in international relations can never be soundly based until the nations that have dispossessed and displaced indigenous peoples accept the precepts of international law that now require a fair accommodation of indigenous peoples in their own nations.

For indigenous peoples in many parts of the world, ANCSA shone as a beacon of hope. The irony is, after serious consideration, they have not used ANCSA as a model. Aware of its flaws, they have rejected any further suggestion of shareholders' corporations and of the taxation of subsistence lands, and they have reaffirmed their conviction that Native lands should be passed intact from one generation to the next.

If governments continue in their efforts to force Native societies into molds that we have cast, I believe they will continue to fail. No tidy bureaucratic plan of action for Native people can have any chance of success unless it takes into account the determination of Native peoples to remain themselves. Their determination to retain their own cultures and their own lands does not mean that they wish to return to the past, it means they refuse to let their future be dictated by others. Because Native peoples have accepted a dominant society's technology does not mean they should learn in school no language except that of the dominant society, learn no history but that of the dominant society, and be governed by no institutions but those of the dominant society. The right of Native peoples to their own distinct place in the contemporary life of the larger nation must be affirmed. At the same time, they must have full access to the social, economic, and political institutions of the dominant society.

The claims of indigenous peoples everywhere cast a beam of light across the pretensions of the world's nations to illuminate in a new way the ideological conflicts that preoccupy them. In this light, we can see how alike the nations are, both East and West. The indigenous peoples of the world are raising profound questions that cannot be answered by technical science, material progress, or representative democracy. All of these questions must be answered in Alaska. The problems are now manifest; the means of resolving them are ready at hand. All that is needed is will, good will.

EPILOGUE

I want to emphasize the moral and the ethical considerations here. I think too often they get forgotten as we discuss the policies and the procedures and the legalities of all of this. We all need to ask ourselves what's right and what's wrong and what's best for the Native people. And I feel that, even though the restoration act is not one hundred percent satisfactory to all members of our tribe, we did something that was never done before in the history of Indian affairs in this country, and that is a grass-roots movement, a major policy reversal, that started at the bottom and then resulted in the passage and the implementation of the Menominee Restoration Act. *(Ada Deer, Menominee Tribe, Wisconsin)*

We often think of Native peoples as curiosities, we consider their reservations squalid, we call the life that many of them lead on urban skid rows deplorable. We regard them as the sad remnants of a culture that is well and truly past. Only their art, handicrafts, carvings, and totem poles survive the wreckage.

Ever since the first Europeans set foot in the New World, Native cultures have been under attack. The Indians, then the Eskimos, were systematically taught to believe that their religions, their languages, their ways of raising children, their whole way of life should be discarded. Although the Natives' enforced retreat has resulted in shocking casualties, they have refused to assimilate. They will not give up their idea of who they are. In the Arctic and sub-Arctic regions of North America, Native identity is essentially linked to subsistence, to the Native economy.

White men who dream of vanquishing the wilderness in the name of industry and progress have led a sustained assault against the Native subsistence economy. Great rivers have been dammed, mines developed, and pipelines built across ancient hunting grounds that once belonged to Eskimos and Indians alone. Industrial man has condemned Native subsistence hunting societies. The only surprising thing about this long history is that we have not succeeded. Remarkably, many of these societies, in defiance of history, still survive; some of them thrive.

But Native people know that they cannot continue to survive unless they have Native governments that exercise political authority and that can defend subsistence. This is the goal that Native people in the villages of Alaska are seeking.

They are aware of the obstacles. They have been told that bureaucrats in the Department of the Interior are opposed to this idea. The State of Alaska is said to be opposed to it. Alaska's congressional delegation is said to be opposed to it. Villagers are told that, remote as they are from lawmakers in Washington, D.C., their goals are impossible to achieve.

Sometimes imagination is stronger than perceived reality. Subjective feelings play a great part in any community's sense of identity. These Native villages, although they have no visible means of influencing the powerful, are nevertheless insisting on their sovereign rights. They believe their future lies in the assertion of their own common identity and the defense of their own common interests. They believe they must be secure in the possession of their land and they must enjoy institutions of self-government that will enable them to defend their land. Religion can be changed; language can be lost; schools and television may arrive—but, as long as they have their land, and as long as they can live off their land, they will be what they are and have always been. For many in government and the bureaucracy, such goals are viewed with great unease.

Governments build castles in the air. They want to believe that building schools in the bush and establishing corporations on the tundra will modernize rural Alaska. But there is no real prospect of wages or salaried employment except for a few persons in each village. The only possibilities for any measure of self-sufficiency lie in access to fish and wildlife. At present, state and federal policies seem designed to limit access to these resources. Is it any wonder the Native peoples are bitter because the promises held out, under the rubrics of education and development, have not been fulfilled? And that now, as they see their land and subsistence rights in jeopardy, they should be insisting on facing truths that others will not face? Who are the realists? Who are the sentimentalists?

Are these Alaska Natives foolish to want what so many say they cannot have? I don't think so. In fact, they may be wiser than the men of affairs who insist their hopes will be dashed. Simply to prop up ANCSA's corporations will do no more than maintain an unacceptable status quo. Given the likelihood of bankruptcies, takeovers, and taxation, given the possibility of greatly reduced federal and state funding in rural Alaska, who can justify the continuation of present arrangements? Only those who are immersed in its minutiae would try to keep going a system that cannot be made to work in village Alaska. All our history and all our experience tell us now what will happen if the land remains a corporate asset. Alaska Natives, like American Indians in the Lower 48 after passage of the General Allotment Act, are going to lose their land. I do not mean that, even at the worst, they will lose their land on the morning of January 1, 1992, but the attrition of land that will begin on that date will continue. Unless changes are made now, there will be no means to check the loss of land later.

These villages have never lived up to the expectations of governments and bureaucrats, who are prone to gloomy predictions about the demise of Native culture: they find it hard to believe that these people can survive. Yet for five hundred years the Native peoples of the Americas have survived attempts to exterminate them, decimation by disease, and efforts by churches and schools to assimilate them. We have always underestimated the Natives' tenacity. Although it is sometimes hard to foresee in the villages a future based on self-sufficiency, I know that the Natives are convinced they will find a way.

Don't they deserve, at least, an opportunity for change on their own terms? This opportunity is the one thing I claim my recommendations will provide: they are based on what the Native peoples told me they want to do for themselves. Too often, we have thought of Native villages as living folk museums or as social laboratories. Why not allow them to become what the Native peoples themselves have in mind? Why not let them evolve in their own way?

Perhaps not all of my recommendations can be quickly implemented, but nothing less than the recommendations made here will enable village Alaska to survive. I have seen the effects of assimilationist policies in the villages. Among some Alaska Natives, there is a feeling of deep, bitter resignation, a sense of irretrievable loss that has weakened the hold of some on their very lives. This sense of loss, of intolerable grievance, has a bearing on the rates of alcoholism, violence, and suicide in rural Alaska. Notwithstanding an undoubted rise in living standards during the past decade, these rates have increased. No one can be certain of the causes of social pathology or of its cures, but it seems reasonable to suppose that if the Native peoples can regain a sense of self-worth, a measure of control over their communities, and an opportunity to make a living off the land, they will have a firm basis for a renewed collective and personal sense of well-being.

Here in rural Alaska is a way of life that contributes to the health of individuals, keeps families on the land, and contributes to the integrity of the village. Yet it is said to be dying because it does not represent our ideas of progress. It is the way of life that the occupation of the West—the great epic of United States history—almost destroyed in the Lower 48. I have met and heard, throughout Alaska, Natives who are determined that the history of the Lower 48 shall not be repeated here. Congress must fully acknowledge for Alaska, as it has done for the Lower 48, the legitimacy of the foundations of Native life. Indian Country must remain Indian Country, Eskimo Country must remain Eskimo Country, Aleut Country must remain Aleut Country.

So my journey ends. It has taken me to places that seem cold and barren in winter, dusty and remote in summer. But here in these villages the encounter that began in 1492 continues. The encounter will not end in Alaska, but the choices that Americans confront there may, in the long sweep of history, provide a unique opportunity to do justice to the Native peoples. It is an opportunity they must not reject.

CHAPTER NOTES

Introduction

Jimmy Stotts, treasurer of the Arctic Slope Regional Corporation at Barrow, gave the figure of $35 million relating to the legal costs incurred in litigation over Section 7(i) of ANCSA, which governs revenue sharing.

One: The Promise of the Claims Act

My account of the Alaska Natives' struggle for a settlement of land claims in Alaska is necessarily cursory. Any full account will have to give more credit to the efforts of persons like William Paul, who pioneered Native claims in Alaska; to the report of the Federal Field Committee for Development Planning in Alaska, *Alaska Natives and the Land* (1968); to the Alaska Federation of Natives (AFN); to Don Wright, president of AFN in 1971, when Congress enacted ANCSA; and to others, such as Willie Hensley and Charlie Edwardsen, Jr. The story has been told in part elsewhere: Mary Clay Berry, *The Alaska Pipeline: The Politics of Oil and Native Land Claims* (Bloomington: Indiana University Press, 1975); James Gallagher, *Etok: A Story of Eskimo Power* (New York: Putnam's, 1974); and Robert D. Arnold, *Alaska Native Land Claims* (Anchorage: Alaska Native Foundation, 1976 and 1978). The figures of $375 and $6,525 came from Arnold (1978, p. 218). A book indicating early doubts about ANCSA is by Frederick Seagayuk Bigjim and James Ito-Adler, *Letters to Howard* (Anchorage, Alaska Methodist University Press, 1975).

I have not, in this chapter, mentioned some of ANCSA's provisions, which, although important, are not essential to an understanding of its effects. It may, however, be useful to some readers if I mention a few here: Native people, insufficient in number (i.e., fewer than twenty-five) to constitute a village, who nevertheless outnumbered non-Natives in their vicinity and constituted at least two families, would be entitled to form a "group" to receive land.

During the first five years after ANCSA, all Natives enrolled within a region received at least ten percent of the money distributed from the Alaska Native Fund through equal amounts of per capita distributions. In addition, each regional corporation had to distribute at least forty-five percent of these funds among its village corporations and at-large shareholders. As a result, during the first five years, shareholders enrolled in village corporations received a per capita share of at least ten percent of each distribution; at-large shareholders received directly a per capita share of at least fifty-five percent because they would not be eligible for dividends or other benefits from a village corporation.

In determining the intent of Congress, I have relied on the provisions of the act and its legislative history. It was not a settlement in the same way that a treaty may be characterized as a settlement; no documents were signed; I have not, therefore, in considering the intent of the act, relied on the goals the Natives may have had.

At the commission's first roundtable, Native leaders who had been active during 1971 characterized ANCSA from the Native side as strictly a real-estate deal. In determining what Alaska Natives generally sought to achieve through ANCSA, I have relied on the evidence they gave before me and on a paper prepared by Ann Fienup-Riordan describing her analysis of the evidence they gave in 1968 and 1969 before congressional committees and subcommittees.

The state-chartered municipal governments in most of the villages in Alaska are classified as second-class cities under Alaska law. I have referred to them as state-chartered local governments, so that I shall not confuse readers unfamiliar with this fact.

ANCSA provided, under Section 14(c)(3), that village corporations are required to convey "at least" 1,280 acres for municipal purposes to state-chartered local governments. In 1980, ANILCA, Section 1405, amended this section to provide that, if the parties agreed, a lesser acreage could be conveyed. This amendment has generally been regarded as requiring "up to" 1,280 acres.

The question of gravel was thought to be settled but is being litigated again by villages that do not accept the settlement worked out by the regional corporations.

An early analysis of the prospects of village corporations is Lee Gorsuch, "Village Corporation Finances," *Alaska Native Management Review*, March 15, 1974. Here is found the suggestion that villages with fewer than six hundred shareholders had little chance of success.

I have made use of the draft *ANCSA 1985 Study*, prepared by ESG, 5201 Leesburg Pike, Falls Church, VA 22041, for the Secretary of the Interior. The material in the draft was assembled by contractors to assist the Secretary in making his "status report" to Congress, as required by ANCSA.

The *ANCSA 1985 Study* bears out my conclusions regarding the village corporations, and it confirms the lack of data. The study, for purposes of financial analysis, divides the village corporations between "surface-rich village corporations" and "surface-poor village corporations." The "surface-rich" corporations received well-timbered lands in 1979–1980. They began to harvest it and revenues increased. As for the "surface-poor" corporations, they are described as "rather static entities," whose revenues do not vary significantly. The increases in 1980 of shareholders' equity are due primarily to the final distributions received from the Alaska Native Fund. Because many of the "surface-poor" corporations did not submit reports to the State of Alaska, they were not included in the analysis. It can, I think, be assumed that most of them for all practical purposes have gone out of business.

As regards regional corporations, this subject is covered in Chapter 18, "Financial Data and Analysis: Regional Corporations," *ANCSA 1985 Study*. The closest approximation to corporate net worth is found in the item "shareholders' equity," described as "the difference between total assets and total liabilities." It includes, as assets, "net property, plant, and equipment," an item that in turn includes land and subsurface rights, both of which are difficult to value. (The data in the *ANCSA 1985 Study* are taken from the annual reports of the regional corporations.) I think that tracing stockholders' equity from the time of incorporation during the early 1970s is likely to give a realistic picture of the true condition of the regional corporations. In most cases, it reveals a steady growth of net worth during the period in which capital was being drawn from the Native Fund and land selections were being made. After that period, certain corporations show a decline in net worth; of course, in some cases, net worth has remained more or less constant after infusions of capital from the fund ceased. But this fact can be misleading because, when the rate of inflation is taken into account, there is a reduction in net worth. In certain other cases, however, there appears to have been a true increase, although Ahtna, Inc. and Cook Inlet Region, Inc. appear to be the only ones that can make such a claim with certainty.

Glenn Fredericks is president of Kuskokwim Corporation, a merger of ten village corporations that acts as consultant to other village corporations.

The quote from Roy Huhndorf is from his article in *The Anchorage Times*, March 4, 1984. The quote from Janie Leask is from her presentation to the Presidential Commission on Indian Reservation Economies.

The suit brought by the Tlingit and Haida is cited as *Tlingit and Haida Indians v. United States*, 177 F. supp. 452 (Ct. Cls. 1959) and 389 F.2nd 778 (Ct. Cls. 1968).

Professor Monroe Price, "ANCSA in Perspective," in John Haines et al., *Minus 31 and the Wind Blowing* (Anchorage: Alaska Pacific University Press, 1980).

With respect to Alaska Native population figures: 80,000 Alaska Natives enrolled under ANCSA, including some who do not live in Alaska. The 1980 census showed 64,000 Alaska Natives in the state, with an estimated 22,500 outside. A good estimate of the current population of Alaska Natives within the state is at least 70,000.

Two: Subsistence

The Act of July 1, 1870, is cited as 16 Stat. 180. The Act of December 29, 1897, is cited as 30 Stat. 226. The *Marine Mammal Protection Act* is cited as 16 U.S.C. 1531 et seq. The *International Whaling Convention* of December 2, 1946, is cited as 62 Stat. 1716, TIAS N. 1849.

The state subsistence law is cited as ch 151 SLA 1978, codified at scattered parts of A.S. 16.05.

In *Carlos Frank v. State*, 604 P.2d 1068 (1979), the Alaska Supreme Court upheld the right to take a moose for an Athabascan funeral potlatch as a right protected under the freedom of religion clause of the First Amendment to the U.S. Constitution and Article I, Section 4 of the Alaskan constitution.

See also Harvey A. Feit, *James Bay Cree Self-Governance and Management of Land and Wildlife under the James Bay and Northern Quebec Agreement*, a paper delivered at the American Indian Workshop of the European Association of American Studies, Copenhagen, April 1985.

The figure regarding the percentage of fish in the Native diet in the Kodiak region comes from the Kodiak Area Native Association subsistence study.

Three: Land

President Jefferson made his intentions clear regarding the removal of the Indians in his secret instructions to William Henry Harrison, February 27, 1803, in which he delineated the true objectives of his Administration.

The story of the Cherokees is well told by Professor Gary C. Anders of the University of Alaska, Juneau, in "The Reduction of the Cherokees, a Self-Sufficient People, to Poverty and Welfare Dependency," in *The American Journal of Economy and Sociology*, July 1981.

As regards the Black Hills, "all difficulty in this matter" has not yet been resolved. In 1980, the U.S. Supreme Court held that the treaty forced on the Sioux by the Grant administration was illegal: *U.S. v. Sioux Nation of Indians*, 448 U.S. 371. See also William S. McFeely, *Grant: A Biography* (New York: Norton, 1981).

The General Allotment Act was not the first of its kind. There had been allotment statutes in the United States during the 1850s, and under them a great deal of Indian land had been alienated. Congress was reminded of this fact while it was considering the General Allotment Act. Congress might also have considered another precedent: the Great Mahele, in Hawaii, between 1848 and 1850. Under pressure from Americans and other Westerners, King Kamehameha III was forced to distribute Hawaiian lands. He tried throughout this process to preserve the rights of the *maka'ainana* (the common people) to their lands, and certain lands remained subject to the rights of Native tenants. In 1850, the Hawaiian legislature authorized the Land Commission to award fee-simple titles to Native tenants. Title was granted only if the claimant submitted a survey of his property and proved that he was actually using and cultivating the land. Most Hawaiians did not comprehend the implications of the new land system, and the Land Commission awarded less than one percent of all the land in Hawaii to commoners. The concept of fee-simple ownership was completely foreign to the Hawaiian population, and many Native Hawaiians lost their lands to enterprising foreigners, most often Americans. By 1890, foreign businessmen owned or leased most of the usable land in Hawaii.

In discussing limited entry, I have relied on a report by Nasser Kamali issued in September 1984 by the Alaska Commercial Fisheries Entry Commission.

In relation to the general subject of this chapter, here are three worthwhile books on White-Native cultural attitudes: Robert F. Berkhofer in *The White Man's Indian* (New York: Vintage, 1979); J.E. Chamberlin, *The Harrowing of Eden: White Attitudes toward North American Indians* (Toronto: Fitzhenry and Whiteside, 1975); William Cronon, *Changes in the Land* (New York: Hill and Wang, 1983).

The claims of Native tribes on the eastern seaboard of the United States have been revived in recent years because early treaties between the Indians and the states were reached in violation of the Indian Non-Intercourse Act 25 U.S.C. 177. The Maine settlement, enacted by Congress in 1980, came about as the result of such a lawsuit. Other claims are being pressed: see *County of Oneida, New York, et al. v. Oneida Indian Nation*, U.S., 105 S. Ct. 1245 (1985).

Tee-Hit Ton v. U.S. is cited as 348 U.S. 272 (1955).

The story of the Menominee termination and restoration is told in Nicholas C. Peroff, *Menominee Drums* (University of Oklahoma Press, 1982).

The phrase regarding the sacredness of aboriginal title is found in many cases beginning with *Mitchel v. U.S.*, 34 U.S. (9 Pet.) 711, 746 (1835), cited with approval as recently as 1985 in *County of Oneida*, supra at 105 S. Ct. 1252.

Four: 1991

The history of the Métis is to be found in Chapter 2 of my *Fragile Freedoms* (Toronto: Clarke, Irwin, 1981).

An account of the Osage headrights is found in Felix S. Cohen, *Handbook of Federal Indian Law* (Charlottesville, Va.: Michie, Bobbs-Merrill, 1982), on pp. 788– 92.

Under an amendment to ANCSA made in 1976, mergers or consolidations prior to December 19, 1991, are not subject to the right of dissenting shareholders to be bought out. Mergers and consolidations do not, however, directly address the questions of share transferability or of preserving the identity of ancestral lands. They may do so indirectly by allowing small village corporations to combine, by creating the possibility of greater economic strength, and perhaps by making it more attractive to shareholders to hold on to their shares. Paradoxically, a larger and economically more viable corporation may become a more inviting target for takeover. Mergers will move the decision-making process yet farther away from individual villages, and the shareholders in each village will become a minority in a larger merged corporation.

Five: A New Direction

An account of the treaty made with the Creeks is found in Herbert Aptheker, *Early Years of the Republic* (New York: International Publishers, 1976).

Jefferson at first drew up a constitutional amendment for the incorporation of Louisiana in the Union. By the time he placed the legislation before Congress, however, he had decided that no such amendment was necessary.

Standard accounts of the removals are found in Francis P. Prucha, *American Indian Policy in the Formative Years: Indian Trade and Intercourse Acts, 1790–1834* (Cambridge: Harvard University Press, 1962); D'Arcy McNickle, *They Came Here First: The Epic of the American Indian* (New York, Harper and Row, 1975).

The reference to the exegesis of Indian Country is based on S. Lyman Tyler, *A History of Indian Policy* (Washington, D.C.: U.S. Department of the Interior, 1973). The Non-Intercourse Act of 1834 provided a statutory definition of Indian Country:

> [A]ll that part of the United States west of the Mississippi, and not within the states of Missouri and Louisiana, or the territory of Arkansas, and, also, that part of the United States east of the Mississippi, and not within any state to which the Indian title has not been extinguished, for the purposes of this act, (shall be) deemed to be the Indian Country.

This definition remained on the books until the general statutory revision of 1874, when it was deleted, westward expansion having made it obsolete. Even so, at least since *Ex Parte Crow Dog*, 109 U.S. 556 (1883), the courts have treated the concept as part of the common law.

There is still controversy regarding the system of elections established by the Indian Reorganization Act. Wilcomb Washburn, in *A Fifty-Year Perspective on the*

Indian Reorganization Act (AAA, 86, 1984), has reviewed the way in which elections were held under the act.

The House Report that explained the extension of certain provisions of the Indian Reorganization Act to Alaska in 1936 noted that it was necessary:

> because of the peculiar nontribal organizations under which the Alaska Natives operate. They have no tribal organizations as that term is understood generally. Many groups which would otherwise be termed "tribes" live in villages which are the bases of their organizations.

The judgments of Chief Justice Marshall may be cited thus: *Johnson, M'Intosh,* 21 U.S. 8 Wheat 543 (1823). *Cherokee Nation v. Georgia,* 30 U.S. (5 Pet.) 1 (1831). *Worcester v. Georgia,* 31 U.S. (6 Pet.) 515 (1832).

The Indian Reorganization Act of 1934 and the Alaska Reorganization Act of 1936 may be cited as Act of June 18, 1934, 48 Stat. 984 (25 U.S.C. 461 et seq.) and Act of May 1, 1936, 49 Stat. 1250 (25 U.S.C. 473a).

In Russell L. Barsh and James Y. Henderson, *The Road* (Berkeley: University of California Press, 1980), there is a very good discussion of John Marshall's judgments. The authors say that his earlier judgment in *Cherokee Nation* has impeded the complete adoption of his more emphatic view of Indian sovereignty expressed in *Worcester.*

Vine Deloria, Jr., and Clifford Lytle, in *The Nations Within: The Past and Future of American Indian Sovereignty* (New York: Pantheon Books, 1984), have provided an account of the passage of the Indian Reorganization Act, what was hoped to be achieved, and what has been achieved under it. The same authors have provided a comprehensive discussion of tribal courts in *American Indians, American Justice* (Austin: University of Texas Press, 1983).

In 1975, Congress established the American Indian Policy Review Commission, composed of three senators, three representatives, and five Indians. The commission delivered its *Final Report* to Congress in 1977. The report, in general, recommends a continuation of the federal policy of protecting and strengthening tribal governments as permanent governmental units in American society. It urged that the legal doctrines on tribal sovereignty and the trust relationship be reaffirmed. It also urged that terminated and non-federally recognized tribes should be eligible for federal recognition and federal services.

In recent years, Congress has passed a series of measures to strengthen the role of tribal governments. The legislation relating to tribal governments in the Lower 48 has consistently included Alaska Native villages. These enactments include the following three measures that have specifically supported the powers of Native governments in Alaska:

(1975) Indian Self-Determination and Education Assistance Act (25 USC 450 et seq.). This act gives Indian tribes the power to contract with federal agencies for services they need.

(1978) Indian Child Welfare Act (25 USC 1901 et seq.). This act confirms tribal jurisdiction over the welfare of Indian children, and it requires that, in custody and adoption cases, state courts must apply federal standards and tribal preferences that favor Indian families for Indian children.

(1982) Indian Tribal Governmental Tax Status Act, Public Law 97-473. This act gives tribal governments substantially the same tax status as state governments under federal income tax laws. It was amended and made permanent in 1984.

Six: Native Sovereignty in Alaska

The suggestion that the Founding Fathers borrowed from the Iroquois Confederacy is made by Bruce E. Johansen, *Forgotten Founders* (Ipswich, Mass.: Gambit Publishers, 1982).

Recent anthropological studies of Arctic communities indicate that traditional methods of governing domestic affairs persist. Traditional patterns of leadership, according to these studies, have contributed to the ability of Native peoples to accommodate the many forces that affect their communities today.

Felix S. Cohen, *Handbook of Federal Indian Law,* published by University of New Mexico Press in 1942, is the seminal treatise in the field of federal Indian law; revised in Felix S. Cohen, *Handbook of Federal Indian Law,* 1982 edition. Two law-school case books are also useful: Getches, Rosenfelt and Wilkinson, *Federal Indian Law: Cases and Materials* (St. Paul, Minn.: West Publishing Co., 1979, Supplement, 1983); Price and Clinton, *Law and the American Indian* (Charlottesville, Va.: The Michie Company, Law Publishers, 1983). For Alaska, of course, the leading work is David S. Case, *Alaska Natives and American Laws* (Fairbanks: University of Alaska Press, 1984).

The idea of federalism was, in 1789, an innovation in political theory. Boorstin calls it, in *The Republic of Technology* (New York: Harper and Row, 1978), "the best symbol of the Founders' experimental spirit" (p. 57).

It is clear that tribal sovereignty will apply to other tribal assets, even if the tribe has no land. In *Johnson v. Chilkat Indian Village,* 357 F. Supp. 384 (D.C. AK. 1978), the federal district court found that Tlingit property concepts applied to a dispute involving rights to tribal property. The court followed decisions of the U.S. Supreme Court that recognized tribal self-regulation and jurisdiction, including *United States v. Wheeler,* 435 U.S. 313 (1978); and *Jones v. Meehan,* 175 U.S. 1 (1899).

Section 16 of the Indian Reorganization Act authorizes tribes and villages to organize and adopt written constitutions and bylaws by a vote of the tribal members. The Secretary of the Interior has the power to approve IRA tribal constitutions. A tribe or village that organizes itself outside the IRA necessarily operates on the basis of inherent sovereignty alone. The federal government may recognize such a traditional government, and it may choose to deal with it, but the Secretary's approval is not necessary to change the constitution or bylaws of a traditional government.

There are advantages to organizing a tribal government under a constitution adopted pursuant to the Indian Reorganization Act. The Secretary cannot revoke its constitution; only the tribe can revoke it. With the exception of the choice of attorney and the fee charged, no other terms of tribal contracts with attorneys are subject to the Secretary's approval. Even the Secretary is prohibited from selling, encumbering, leasing, or disposing of tribal lands and assets without first obtaining the consent of the tribe; and, finally, members of the tribe are specifically entitled to Bureau of Indian Affairs employment preference.

One of the goals of the Indian Reorganization Act was to limit the Secretary's discretion, which was nearly unrestrained before 1934. The act returned some of these powers to the tribes, and it placed statutory limits on others. In the present climate favorable to self-determination, Secretaries of the Interior have generally dealt with traditional tribes and IRA councils in about the same way.

Under various statutes and programs, the Secretary is required to deal with tribal officers. The Secretary may decline to deal with officers of either IRA councils or traditional tribes, if they are elected in violation of tribal constitution or laws, or in violation of the Indian Civil Rights Act of 1968. Many IRA constitutions, especially those adopted initially, provided for secretarial review of virtually every major tribal decision. In recent years the Secretary has sometimes approved constitutional amendments to eliminate federal review, except where trust property is involved.

In 1958, Congress extended PL 280 to all Indian Country in Alaska, an act that extended state court jurisdiction over the adjudication of civil and criminal matters involving Natives in Indian Country. The main current of opinion is that this left tribal (village) jurisdiction intact, making it concurrent with the jurisdiction of Alaska state courts. No court decision, however, has directly addressed this question. Moreover, a specific provision of PL 280 requires state courts to adjudicate civil disputes between Natives according to the customs and ordinances of the tribe, as long as they are "not inconsistent" with state law. In 1970, the Metlakatla Reservation was exempted from some of the criminal jurisdiction provisions of the act, and specifically afforded concurrent jurisdiction with the state over misdemeanors.

The Spud Williams quote is from his letter to Alaska's Governor Sheffield, October 6, 1983. The quote from Professor Chamberlin is from *Alaska Native News*, September 1984.

All of the materials discussed here are found in David H. Getches, Daniel M. Rosenfelt, and Charles F. Wilkinson, *Cases and Materials on Federal Indian Law* (St. Paul, Minn.: West Publishing Co., 1979). For a discussion of recent developments, see Charles Wilkinson, "Shall the Islands be Preserved?", in *The American West*, Vol. 16, No. 3, May–June, 1979.

Seven: Recommendations

Third parties with bona fide claims against village corporations must be protected. It may be that Congress should appropriate funds to pay off these debts, of which no one knows the full extent. Congress could direct that reimbursement to the Treasury be made by assigning any future revenues the village would otherwise be entitled to receive under Section 7(j) of ANCSA. In this way, a village that had no indebtedness would not be penalized; the Treasury would be repaid out of revenues accruing to the villages that had incurred debts.

Lands for the Native people of Haines, Seward, Wrangell, Petersburg, and Ketchikan could be allocated out of the special purpose lands under Section 14(h) of ANCSA.

If lands are transferred out of regional corporation ownership without compensation, then the revenue-sharing provisions of ANCSA Section 7(i) seem, by their terms, not to apply to revenue received from these lands by the new owner. This means, among other things, that there would be no 7(i) revenue from such a regional corporation for village distribution under Section 7(j).

Professor Ralph Johnson of the College of Law, University of Washington, presented a paper to the Commission stating it as his opinion that Congress has the power to authorize conveyance of ANCSA lands to tribal governments without regard to the rights of dissenting shareholders (such legislation would not violate the Fifth Amendment) and that tribal governments could claim sovereign immunity with respect to such lands, whether they are held in federal trust or not. The same opinion is widely held by other legal experts in the field.

Conservation easements are now commonplace in the Lower 48. A landowner will grant an easement in perpetuity to a conservation organization or to a public agency. Under the federal Internal Revenue Code, the owner obtains a deduction against income on the basis of a charitable contribution. He can retain certain rights to develop mineral resources (oil and gas, deep mining) that do not significantly impair the surface, without jeopardizing the tax write-off.

In Alaska, Native corporations could grant subsistence easements in perpetuity to tribal governments for the benefit of tribal members. The right of tribal members to use the land would be written into the easement. Any change in ownership would not affect the subsistence rights of tribal members. It might be necessary to pass state legislation to enable the easement to be enforced. A ruling would have to be obtained from the Department of the Treasury acknowledging that a tribal government is a qualified organization, for tax purposes, to hold such an easement. See "A Private Sector Strategy to Protect Native Land and Ensure Economic Opportunity," Jan Konigsberg, unpublished paper on file with the Alaska Native Review Commission, May 1985.

Passenger Fishing Vessel Owners Association v. Washington is cited as 443 U.S. 658 (1979).

Regarding Native ownership of waters in Alaska: the aboriginal title of the Inupiat to offshore areas beyond the boundaries of Alaska was still being litigated in 1985. In *Inupiat Community of the Arctic Slope v. U.S.*, 746 F.2d 572 (9th Cir. 1984), the circuit court of appeals denied the Inupiat claim to title and jurisdiction over sea ice, water, and submerged lands beyond the three-mile limit of Alaska's territorial sea. The Inupiat have filed a petition for writ of certiorari to the U.S. Supreme Court, which at this writing is still pending.

Eight: The Fourth World

In its 1984 report on Nicaragua, *Report on the Situation of Human Rights of a Segment of the Nicaraguan Population of Miskito Origin,* the Inter-American Human Rights Commission has chosen a title which sidesteps the vital issue in the case.

Lewis Hanke's works, especially *Aristotle and the American Indians* (Chicago: Henry Regnery Company, 1959), reveal the continuing influence of Bartolomé de Las Casas.

The Norwegian Sami Rights Committee, in its 1984 report, has recommended that a Sami Parliament, similar to the Sami Parliament in Finland, be established in Norway, but the committee was divided on what electoral system should be used. The committee also recommends that Sami committees be set up in municipalities and counties that have a Sami population to serve in an advisory capacity.

The Sub-Commission on the Prevention of Discrimination and the Protection of

Minorities reports to the Commission on Human Rights, which reports to the Economic and Social Council, which reports to the General Assembly. The report authorized in 1971 was completed in 1984.

Professor Douglas Sanders has covered much of the ground of this chapter in D. E. Sanders, "The Re-emergence of Indigenous Questions in International Law," *Canadian Human Rights Yearbook*, 1983. See also Russel L. Barsh, "The International Legal Status of Native Alaska," *Alaska Native News*, July 1984. In *Rethinking Indian Law* (National Lawyers Guild, Committee on Native American Struggles, 1982), it is argued that domestic law has failed Native Americans and they are urged to turn to international law and remedies.

The Helsinki Accords are not technically a treaty, but the United States has been a committee participant in the ongoing process of improving human rights inaugurated under the accords.

Forrest Gerard's testimony on the application of Article VIII to the self-determination of Native Americans appears in "Bulletin Three: Implementation of the Helsinki Accords." Hearings before the Commission on Security and Cooperation in Europe: Human Rights, April 3 and 4, 1979 at 454.

Regarding the history of Soviet policies toward Native peoples, see O. I. Natufe, *The Concept of Native Self-Government in the Soviet North* (Ottawa: Department of Indian and Northern Affairs, 1979).

A declaration by the General Assembly of the United Nations would not automatically become international law because the General Assembly is not an international legislature. The standards contained in the declaration could become international law in two ways: (1) by coming to be regarded as a statement of the accepted principles of nation-states and thus part of customary international law; or (2) by being enshrined in a covenant or treaty that is signed by nation-states, thereby becoming part of "conventional" international law: international law established by conventions or treaties binding on the states that have signed them.

A major part of the developments on the international scene has been international activities of the indigenous peoples themselves. In the mid-1970s, indigenous peoples formed the International Indian Treaty Council and the World Council of Indigenous Peoples. The Inuit Circumpolar Conference was established in 1977. These organizations have been recognized as Non-Governmental Organizations by the Economic and Social Council of the United Nations, which regards them as legitimate international organizations, capable of assisting the United Nations in its continuing work.

The refusal to concede that Indians remained distinct was characteristic of Latin American countries. The great Indian president of Mexico, Benito Juárez, opposed the idea of Indianness.

The concept of self-determination was first applied after World War I to redraw the boundaries of Europe after the breakup of the German, Austro-Hungarian, and Turkish empires. Where national boundaries could not be redrawn along cultural and linguistic lines, the peace treaties included provisions to protect specific minorities within the European nations. There was no assertion of a principle of self-determination or of minority rights, but here was the beginning of an international law for minorities. The League of Nations and the Permanent Court of International Justice (predecessor of the International Court of Justice) supervised these treaties. The charter of the United Nations includes a commitment to an international law of "human rights and fundamental freedoms," an idea that led to the Universal Declaration of Human Rights in 1949.

APPENDIX:

THE ALASKA NATIVE

REVIEW COMMISSION

In July 1983, the Inuit Circumpolar Conference established the Alaska Native Review Commission and appointed the Honorable Thomas R. Berger to be commissioner.

The Inuit Circumpolar Conference, founded in June 1977, is an organization of Alaskan, Canadian and Greenlandic Inuit (Eskimo) governments and associations concerned with environmental protection, national economic development, and indigenous self-determination in the Arctic.

In December 1983, the World Council of Indigenous Peoples, which represents the interests of Native peoples in North and South America and of indigenous peoples on other continents, became co-sponsor of the Alaska Native Review Commission.

The commission's terms of reference are to examine and report on:

1. The socio-economic status of Alaska Natives

2. The history and intent of the Alaska Native Claims Settlement Act, 1971 (ANCSA)

3. The historic policies and practices of the United States in settling the claims of Native Americans, placing ANCSA in political perspective

4. The functions of the various Native corporations in fulfilling the "spirit" of ANCSA for Alaska Natives

5. The social, cultural, economic, political, and environmental significance of ANCSA to indigenous people around the world

The Commission was directed to present a report and to make recommendations.

Roundtable Discussions

To provide an intellectual framework for consideration of the broad issues involved, the commission held a series of roundtable discussions in Anchorage during February and March 1984, with the following objectives:

1. To identify the expectations that Alaska Natives had, prior to ANCSA, for a settlement of their claims and the values they sought to protect, and to examine the moral and ethical principles upon which their claims are founded

2. To evaluate the effects of changes in land tenure and of traditional land use on the lives of Alaska Natives, on relations between the Native peoples and the state, and on their present expectations with regard to ANCSA

3. To review the history of the United States federal policies and practices toward Native Americans and to ANCSA, and to review implications for the future

4. To evaluate the applicability of ANCSA to indigenous people in other states

and other nations who are struggling to secure a settlement and land and to secure self-determination, and to bring the experience of these peoples to bear on the situation in Alaska

A later series of roundtable discussions was held during 1984 and 1985 to examine specific issues.

1. Subsistence. To examine and clarify the subsistence values of Alaska Natives, regulatory regimes and their impacts, considerations affecting subsistence, and other possibilities

2. ANCSA and 1991. To assess problems and deficiencies identified in ANCSA legislation, such as the exclusion of Natives born after 1971, the prospects of taxation and of stock transfers after 1991, and to consider possible remedies

3. Alternative approaches to Native land and governance. To identify and evaluate underlying causes of concern and to consider the viability of present and other possible approaches to, and institutions for, Native landholding and governance, as may be evident in Alaska, the United States, Canada, and elsewhere, and to suggest adjustments in the relationships with federal, state, and local regimes

4. The place of Native peoples in the Western world. To consider the place of aboriginal peoples, both historically and in contemporary terms, in relation to dominant Western ideologies and institutions and to evaluate the grounds on which they are making claims to ancestral lands and for greater autonomy

Documentation

All public hearings and roundtable discussions were recorded, and verbatim transcripts have been produced in ninety-five volumes and on microfiche. An index, audiotapes, and a number of edited videotape programs of commission meetings are available. Information about them may be obtained from the Inuit Circumpolar Conference, 429 D Street, Suite 211, Anchorage, Alaska 99501. Telephone (907) 338-6917.

Village Hearings

The Alaska Native Review Commission held public hearings in these villages and cities in this order: Emmonak, Tununak, Copper Center, Gulkana, University of Alaska at Fairbanks, Fairbanks, Nenana, Tanacross, Juneau, Sitka, Angoon, Ketchikan, Saxman, Klawock, Hydaburg, Metlakatla, Point Hope, Holy Cross, Galena, Huslia, Akiachak, fish camps (Kuskokwim River), Stevens Village, fish camps (Yukon River), Rampart, Tanana, Barrow, Anaktuvuk Pass, Seward, Tatitlek, Eyak (Cordova), Kenai, Port Graham, English Bay, Sand Point, Unalaska, Akutan, Nome, Gambell, Shishmaref, Unalakleet, Klukwan, Haines, Kotzebue, Shungnak, Selawik, Tyonek, Kodiak, Larsen Bay, Fort Yukon, Venetie, St. George, St. Paul, New Stuyahok, Togiak, Newhalen, Anchorage, Dillingham, Aniak, Sleetmute, Bethel, and Seattle.

THOMAS R. BERGER was born in 1933 in Victoria, British Columbia, Canada. He studied law at the University of British Columbia and practiced law in Vancouver until he was appointed to the British Columbia Supreme Court in 1971. He was the youngest judge to sit on that court in this century.

Berger has headed royal commissions of inquiry under each of Canada's three major political parties. In 1973–1974, he undertook the Commission on Family and Children's Law for the New Democratic government of British Columbia.

From 1974 to 1977, under the Liberal government of Prime Minister Pierre Trudeau, Berger headed the Mackenzie Valley Pipeline Inquiry to determine the social, environmental, and economic impact of the proposed Arctic Gas pipeline to be built from Prudhoe Bay in Alaska down through the Mackenzie Valley in western Canada. In 1977, the government of Canada rejected the Arctic Gas pipeline proposal on Berger's recommendation. For his work as commissioner of the Mackenzie Valley Pipeline Inquiry, Berger received a distinguished achievement award from the Sierra Club of North America in 1978, and was named an honorary member of the Engineering Institute of Canada in 1979. *Northern Frontier, Northern Homeland,* the report of Berger's commission, was the best-selling book ever published by the government of Canada.

In 1979, Berger headed a third commission, under the Conservative government of Prime Minister Joe Clark, this time dealing with Indian and Inuit health-care programs. Berger has been widely credited with using royal commissions as a powerful new force in the Canadian political process.

In 1981, Berger's public intervention (personally opposed by Prime Minister Trudeau) was instrumental in the inclusion of aboriginal rights in the new Canadian constitution. That same year, he wrote *Fragile Freedoms,* a study of human rights and dissent in Canada.

In April 1983, Berger resigned from the bench in order to be free to speak on questions of human rights. In August 1983, he was chosen to head the Alaska Native Review Commission in Anchorage. It was sponsored by two international organizations of aboriginal peoples, the Inuit Circumpolar Conference and the World Council of Indigenous Peoples. His report is contained in the present volume.

Berger holds honorary degrees from twelve universities and has lectured widely in Canada and the U.S. He is currently professor of law at the University of British Columbia in Vancouver. He is married to Beverley Crosby, and has a daughter, Erin, and a son, David.